PORT
an Introduction to its History and Delights

CHRISTMAS 1984
OUR LOVE,
DAD AND LINDA ANN

PORT

an Introduction to
its History and Delights

WYNDHAM FLETCHER

SOTHEBY PARKE BERNET

© W. J. S. Fletcher   1978

First published 1978 for
Sotheby Parke Bernet Publications
by Philip Wilson Publishers Ltd.,
Russell Chambers, Covent Garden, WC2

USA edition available from
Biblio Distribution Center,
81 Adams Drive, Totowa, New Jersey 07512

ISBN 0 85667 044 8

Designed by Lynn Lewis
End papers by David Gentleman
Illustrations in *Reminiscences* chapter by Edward Ardizzone

Printed and bound in Great Britain by
Butler and Tanner Limited, Frome

Cockburn Smithes & Company Limited, shippers of Port wine since 1815, are delighted to have contributed to the production of this valuable book on one of the great wines of the world, with financial support, photographs and other illustrations.

Contents

Foreword

Port, we are sometimes reminded, has traditionally been known as 'the Englishman's wine', a resounding affirmation that could conceal a thrust at the Scots for their alleged preference for that 'less than manly French stuff, claret'. Yet perhaps Port owes no little of its success indirectly to the French. For it was the Anglo-French rivalry, breaking into open warfare every so often, that, as Wyndham Fletcher mentions in his opening chapter, gave Port, along with other Iberian wines, the edge over the French. This commercial and political rivalry began in the reign of Charles II, was accentuated by William III, and reached an economic warfare pitch with the Methuen Treaty of 1703, the year before the battle of Blenheim. The advantage given to Port was not only in the stipulation that the duty on French wines must be at least one-third higher – a preference that actually lasted until 1831 and at times was much higher – but also in the implication that it was unpatriotic, a sentiment used more recently against German wines in the First World War. In the Napoleonic wars it was surely in Port that well-fed gentlemen drank 'damnation to Boney'; both rhetorically and alcoholically it would have been a good deal less effective in claret.

Yet the French have the laugh on us, as today they drink much more Port than we do, to our shame, although those who accept a pre-prandial 'Porto' in France may usually feel that in quality we still have the best of the bargain. The pioneers, first in Viana and then in Oporto, were later followed by the Sandemans, Taylors and the Cockburns – the last-named having the good fortune to be founded in 1815, the famous 'Waterloo Port' vintage. Their monument is the splendid Factory House in Oporto, the last of such in the world, where I have had the honour to lunch, passing thereafter to the second dining-room where the Port is circulated.

This book may suggest a traditional, leisurely way of life, and such is associated with Port, nowadays often unfairly, to its disadvantage. It is true that the engaging picture Wyndham Fletcher draws of the Cockburn office in the City of London in the 1930s does not exactly evoke the sense of entrepreneural activity, marketing techniques and case-sale statistics that, necessarily enough, occupy the wine trade today; including those 'in Port'. However, as the earlier chapters of this book show, the making of Port has always been highly skilled, and the gentlemen who passed the Port, both in the Factory House and Mark Lane, had to work hard for their living, and as in other parts of the wine trade, even 'the partners' were seldom as well-off as the opulence of their wares might suggest.

It must be admitted, however, that the traditional image of Port did not fit in with the post-World War I scene, when young Wyndham first hung up his bowler hat in 60, Mark Lane, although a few years later a prodigious amount of

Port was being consumed in Britain – not in Pall Mall clubs but in the Private and Saloon bars of pubs, where working-class women foregathered to enjoy their Port and lemon. In those days, not so long ago, as he mentions, brand names in Wood Port were almost unknown, with the exception of Sandeman, who in certain circles were not thought all the better for this blatant piece of self-advertisement. In Vintage Port, yes, names were important – although, in fact, this only came about around 1870, before which Port usually bore the name of the importing retail merchant who bottled it.

Consequently while Wyndham Fletcher's expert account of Port may suggest an easy life, the post-World War II epoch in the trade has had many problems; and that he himself became one of the most respected figures in it was the result of hard work. Cockburn, of course, has always occupied a special place in the canon of Port firms, and the author's predecessors, Ernest and Fred Cockburn, were notable figures too. The former was before my time, but I knew the latter some years before he retired; a jovial, gregarious personality. Among Vintage Port drinkers Cockburn has always had a reputation for going its own way in choosing which vintages to declare. For example they did not offer 1897 as some firms did, more, it was suggested, on account of Queen Victoria's Jubilee than the quality of the wine, for they had already declared 1896. Then there was the extraordinary jump between 1912 and 1927, whereas, as can be seen in the appendix at the end of this book, others shipped 1917, 1920, 1922 and 1924; and some even 1919. In the controversial choice that must have shaken the Factory House to its very solid foundations, as to whether to declare the 1934 or the 1935, Cockburn chose the latter year. Doubtless they would still be arguing about it in Mark Lane luncheon rooms if the Germans had not so ineptly destroyed the centre of the English wine trade and scattered it for ever.

After that war, Cockburn declared 1947 rather than the more usual 1948, though they were not alone in that, but stood out more prominently twenty years later in foregoing the almost universally offered 1966 and instead declared 1967, along with their then fairly new associated firm, Martinez.

The last vintage declared when Wyndham was associated with Cockburn was 1975, and on the occasion of its introduction in 1977, he organised a splendid tasting that I attended in London of Cockburn and Martinez vintages going back to 1890. This 87-year-old Cockburn Port looked like madeira and tasted rather like it, as very old Port often does, but it had no decay, though the spirit was showing. It was superior, in my view, to the Martinez 1896 that followed. 1908 and 1912 were two famous years whose comparative merits were canvassed for many years. As Wyndham Fletcher wrote in his notes on the tasting card, 'In my time in the trade, first one and then the other has been considered the greater classic. 1908 is lighter and perhaps a little finer than 1912 which was bigger and more robust!' I myself opted for the '08, and was glad to find that he did also, though in general the '12 has usually been thought to have had an advantage over its elder. Then came the celebrated '27, which, as Wyndham Fletcher says, now fetches exceptionally high prices in the London saleroom, reaching £310 a dozen in 1977 at Sotheby's. It showed beautifully full and fruity, rather putting the accompanying Martinez in the shade, but then other notable '27s have been showing their spirit for some time. The succeeding '35 was at its peak, Vintage Port at its best and most complete after forty years in bottle. Cockburn, unfortunately perhaps, did not ship the '45, and the '47 was agreeable but not very distinguished, and the following '50 lacked character to my way of thinking. However, the '55 more than made up for this, with enormous colour and fruit and so much 'behind it' that surely Cockburn '55 will last well into the twenty-first century. Of the rest of the vintages shown – '60, '63, '67 and '70 – there is less to be said now, except that today Cockburn '60 is a very agreeable, ready-to-drink Port, the '63 is another very powerful wine, and the '67 much lighter. However, John Smithes, whose father made the '27, held the view that this '67 would turn out 'another 1927'. *On verra!*

Perhaps, in this foreword I have written too much about the wine and its ambiance and too little about Wyndham and his book. However, as this shows, he is a notably modest man and his book needs no bush. All the details of Port production are set forth simply but expertly, and written by someone with long experience and inside knowledge. The history is sketched in lightly, and the account of his own years in the trade will be of value to the social historian and the student. Above all, one has the gratifying feeling that he really knows his wine, an essential element in all writing on an elusive subject, and that he *enjoys* it.

EDMUND PENNING-ROWSELL   FEBRUARY 1978

Preface

When I was invited to write this book I accepted with pleasure, although with some hesitation, since I am not practised in the art of authorship, nor do I consider myself one of those sometimes described as 'an expert on Port'. However, my working life has been spent in the trade and consequently, in conjunction with many visits to Portugal, including an initial stay of a year, I have been able to acquire a fair knowledge of wine-making. My many good friends in the business have filled the gaps in my viticultural education and kept me up-to-date with everchanging and developing modern techniques. I thank them all for their patience in answering my questions.

I would like to take this opportunity of expressing gratitude to my old colleagues who have taught me so much – Reggie Cobb, Fred Cockburn, John Smithes, Colin Gordon, Felix Vigne and the late Frank Ree. My thanks are due to all the authors of the books I have consulted during my research, particularly Sarah Bradford whose brilliant book *The Englishman's Wine* has been of immense help. I must also mention the very great assistance I have derived from being allowed to quote freely from the most valuable paper on the Douro by Exmo. Snr. José Antonio Rosas of Adriano Ramos-Pinto, Vila Nova de Gaia.

To Sotheby's Master of Wine, Patrick Grubb, I am greatly indebted for his valuable help throughout the preparation of my book and also to my friends at Harvey's for their sponsorship and for providing all the illustrations.

I hope this book will be of interest to all those who are already confirmed Port drinkers and will encourage and enlighten all those who are new to the Port world.

WYNDHAM FLETCHER   1978

Portugal and Port

To the Portuguese, even in these turbulent and changing times, the association with this country as 'England's oldest ally' is valued to this day. English crusaders helped in the capture of Lisbon from the Moors in the twelfth century, in the reign of the first King of Portugal, Afonso Henriques, though they were said to be given to various unfortunate excesses when under the influence of the local wine. This early involvement between the two countries led to a Treaty of Perpetual Friendship in 1373 and it was this treaty which, though Portugal was neutral, was invoked by Churchill in 1943 to allow us to use the Azores as a naval and air base and which, after some argument, was duly honoured. I remember mentioning this to a friend who was a Royal Marine in the last war. 'Ah, yes,' he said, 'I was in a Marine battalion embarked in a cruiser with another battalion in another ship in company; we were hull down off the island during the negotiations – just in case!' As Churchill said, the House of Commons was very suitably impressed that a treaty of such antiquity was adhered to and still carried weight.

In 1973 there were great celebrations in London for the 600th anniversary of the treaty, and the then Prime Minister of Portugal, Dr. L. Caetano, came over for the occasion as the guest of the British Prime Minister, Edward Heath. I was lucky enough to be at that moment Chairman of the Port Wine Trade Association, so that my wife and I were much involved in the celebrations. There was an opening dinner in the Painted Hall at Greenwich, followed by lunches at the Mansion House and Lancaster House and an evening reception.

Towards the end of the fifteenth and early in the sixteenth centuries, at the time of the famous Portuguese navigators, there was a great increase in trade between the two countries, largely in codfish and in wine. At that time wines of quality came from the Lisbon area, both north and south of the Tagus, and the northern wines of the Minho shipped through Viana do Castelo near the Spanish frontier were not highly regarded, being thought thin and astringent.

The next historical milestone came with the advent of Cromwell's Commonwealth. The then King of Portugal, João IV, who had reluctantly ascended the throne in 1640, naturally rather resented the removal of a brother monarch's head, as an infringement of trade practice, and this resentment was fuelled by the presence in the Tagus of a royalist squadron under Prince Rupert. Cromwell wanted to send in Blake's fleet to flush out the royalists, but eventually Rupert was persuaded by the Portuguese to remove himself and his ships. The restoration of relations with the Commonwealth led to the signing of a commercial treaty in 1654 giving English merchants a privileged position in Portugal and 'most favoured nation' terms in trade generally. This really established the close commercial relationship between the two countries and laid the foundations of the trade which has lasted to this day.

About this time Portugal was having one of her periodic differences of opinion with Spain and a story (unverified) of English troops sent by Cromwell to help his new ally bears repetition. A New Model regiment arrived in Lisbon with instructions to the Colonel to report to the Portuguese Commander and to place himself under his orders. The Colonel and his regiment eventually found the Portuguese drawn up on a hill near the frontier, with the Spanish on another hill across the valley. The Portuguese General, being asked what his intentions were, gave the impression of waiting on developments. Whereupon the Englishman, in typical 'damn their eyes' style, launched his regiment at the enemy and drove them off the hill in rout. The Portuguese General, turning to his staff, remarked sadly, "These heretics are worth more to us than all our saints."

The trade firmly established with the Commonwealth received a great fillip at the time of the wars with Louis XIV. French protectionist policy led to retaliation in the banning of French wines and a great increase in the demand for 'Red Portugal', handled by the English now in residence. Moreover it was discovered that the wines of the Douro were fuller and had more body than the thin Minho wines, and were therefore more to the English taste. In 1678 the first entry was inscribed in the Oporto Custom House of 'Vinho do Porto', shipped over the bar of the Douro. By the end of the century many thousands of pipes of Port wine were being shipped annually and coopers were sent out from

England to teach their craft to the Portuguese. Like the earliest Crusaders, though probably with more excuses, there were problems with the influence of the local wine.

The next landmark was the Methuen Treaty of 1703, whereby Portugal took English wool free of duty and England gave a preferential duty of a third on Portuguese wines against French imports. Contrary to general belief, this concession did not have any immediate effect on shipments, which were already running at a high level. In 1727 the British Association was formed from the British Factory or Trading Factors, and the Factory House was completed in 1790. Both the British Association and the Factory House are very much in evidence to this day.

By the middle of the eighteenth century, members of the Factory were complaining of growers in the Douro adding brandy during fermentation, and worse still, *baga* and sugar to cheap wine. *Baga* is a sweet concentrate made of elderberries, the use of which has been banned in wine-making, which is why no elderberry trees may be grown in the Douro district. The growers, in rage and in retaliation, sent a deputation to Lisbon to wait on the Marquis de Pombal, the virtual dictator of Portugal. They utterly refuted the Factory House allegation, and furthermore stated that the prices offered by the members were far too low. The Marquis acted at once by setting up a Wine Monopoly, the 'Old Company', Companhia Geral da Agricultura dos Vinhos do Alto Douro, to control quality and through which all wine had to be bought at fixed prices. He also fixed for the first time the boundaries of the delimited Douro district which, with occasional modifications (the final major ones being made by João Franco in 1907 and 1908, with very minor ones in 1921) have endured to this day, thereby acknowledging the unique qualities of the wines produced. However, political interference with the trade set an unfortunate precedent and came at a time when cheap spirits had become for the first time readily available, with the results depicted by Hogarth. The inefficiency and graft of the monopoly led to it being as heartily disliked by the growers as by the shippers, and the death of the Marquis de Pombal was followed by a gradual relaxation of control.

The end of the eighteenth century saw large quantities of Port being shipped, and the evolution of the modern cylindrical-shaped bottle made it possible to mature wine. The wines were made from the pre-phylloxera national grape, big, heavy and generous, to an extent sometimes fortified, but probably in the main of natural strength. Port, as an acceptable wine, had definitely arrived.

The Peninsular War fought in Portugal between 1807 and 1811 gave considerable impetus to the trade, Wellington's officers, including many sprigs of the nobility, providing it with a fashionable cachet. Another military anecdote, for which there is no confirmation, relates that the 11th Hussars (then the 11th Light Dragoons, now the Royal Hussars) do not owe their nickname of 'The Cherry Pickers' to Lord Cardigan's sartorial vagaries but to a ribald comment by their army comrades when a squadron was surprised by the French while picking cherries in an orchard in north Portugal.

Many of the great shippers' names made their appearance about this time and certainly, by the third and fourth decades of the nineteenth century, tawny (and white) Port had been evolved and were in demand.

In 1831 there arrived in Oporto, as a young man, J. J. Forrester, probably the most fascinating character in the history of the Port trade. Naturalist, cartographer, viticulturist and above all the author, in 1844, of *A Word or Two on Port Wine*, which was in fact a plea for a return to the making of Port in the old way, the must fermented right out, without the addition of brandy. A bitter battle ensued with the rest of the shippers ranged against Forrester, and fortunately no doubt for the future of the trade, he lost the day. He accepted his defeat, was created a baron in the nobility of Portugal, and was then mysteriously drowned in the Cachão rapids of the River Douro while wearing a heavy belt full of gold sovereigns.

By about 1840 the modern method of making Port with the retention of sugar in the fermenting must by the addition of wine brandy was in general use, and in 1858 the monopoly of the 'Old Company' was formally abolished.

Trade was generally good and all was going well until about 1868, when the Douro region, like the rest of Europe, was hit by the phylloxera aphid from America. The 1878 is generally considered to have been the last pre-phylloxera vintage and, for those lucky enough to have tasted it, an experience not to be forgotten. The discovery that American vine-stocks were immune to the aphid, and that the native stocks could be grafted on to them, saved the vineyards and a slow recovery began.

Post-phylloxera vintages started to be shipped in the 1880s and were found to be acceptable to the trade and public; though there seems to be little doubt that these and subsequent wines did not have quite the body or lasting power of the vintages produced from the old national ungrafted vines. But this may be by no means a bad thing with present tastes and commercial conditions.

At the beginning of 1892 occurred an event unique in the annals of the Port wine trade, the Burnay sale. For some time there had been rumours in Mark Lane, the hub of the wine trade, of a spectacular purchase of Port in Oporto for sale by public auction.

These rumours were soon confirmed and it was stated that 17,000 pipes had been bought by Southard & Co. for an unknown account, to be auctioned in London. Later it transpired that the deal had been financed by the Lisbon bankers, H. Burnay & Co., and the head of the firm, Count Burnay arrived in London where he was interviewed by the Press. Apart from the financial backing, the whole business was the brain-child of, and carried through by, Messrs. Southard and Colbeck of Southard's.

So far as Burnay was concerned the idea was to buy silver in London from the profits on the sale of the wine. This would be sold at a profit to the Portuguese Government, to whom the scheme was attractive as they intended to use the bullion for coinage after the wines had been bought in depressed paper currency. Southard's having bought the wines would receive a purchasing commission on the sale in England.

Mr. Colbeck, who had gone to Oporto, approached most of the leading firms, from many of whom he bought parcels at good prices, though in no case under the shipper's brand. His purchase price was, however, averaged-out by buying quantities in the Douro direct from farmers at low prices.

By May Southard's had arranged to offer 10,000 pipes at auction, and samples were available for tasting. C. D. Cobb of Cockburn reported as follows: 'I have just come in from a long tasting at Portal's office of Burnay's wines and can safely say they are a most miserable lot, and I feel sure will only sell at extremely low rates. Of course there are a few decent wines, but very few.'

The first sale was a fair success, though not all the quantity offered was disposed of. However, this was hardly to be wondered at, in view of a surprise sale at about the same time of 1,600 pipes of Croft's Port.

This sale had in fact nothing at all to do with Croft's in Oporto, but represented the whole London stock of their agents Gonne Croft & Co., which was pledged to the firm's bankers, who, being afraid that the Burnay sale might depreciate their security, had ordered the wines to be put up for auction.

The Southard's sales continued with varying but on the whole fair success, and in September 1894 8,000 pipes were offered with the douceur that any wine bought by firms in Oporto could be shipped back at a special freight of ten shillings a pipe arranged by Southard.

The last word so far as Cockburn's were concerned came as late as 1897 when in May, Moncrieff Cockburn wrote 'I tasted all the Burnay wines yesterday and think them a very poor lot.' This must refer to any small parcels then remaining.

But, in spite of all the criticism, it is probable that the effect of the Burnay sales on the Port trade was beneficial. Everyone was talking about Port and making bets about the success of the venture, even as far away as New York. It showed the great strength of the trade in that the introduction of about 17,000 pipes into the country, on top of the ordinary regular shipments, had no appreciable effect on the market. It is perhaps a chastening thought that 17,000 pipes represents approximately the total yearly duty-paid clearances in this country today.

Business prospered through Victorian and Edwardian times right up to the First World War, stimulated by a succession of great classic vintages. In the two decades before 1914, Port became the wine most drunk by the working-class in the pubs, especially by the female element who enjoyed it, to a great extent as a 'Port and lemon' – a glass of ruby Port with a bottle of fizzy lemonade. It was no unusual thing for a hogshead or even a pipe to be sold by the glass over the counter in one week in some East End pubs.

Compared with today, there were a vast number of independent brewers and wine merchants up and down the country, most of whom would bottle several 'marks' of Wood Port, largely under their own label.

In 1914 and 1916 Anglo–Portuguese commercial treaties were signed protecting the word 'Port' both in the country of production, the delimited Douro district of Portugal, and in the country of consumption, Great Britain. This protection was unique in law until comparatively recently, when legal judgements extended this protection of nomenclature to other wines.

In 1919, with freedom of shipping, the great Port boom began, when more Port was shipped to this country than ever before or since. But, like all booms, it carried within itself the seeds of its own decay. War and taxation, as always, formed and changed habits of life, and the arrival of the Americans had started the fashion for pre-meal drinking leading to the cocktail vogue, and then to the fashion for sherry parties. All this on an empty stomach led to a certain sense of satiety when the Port should have been circulating after dinner. Moreover, at the cheaper end of the trade, the Budget of 1927 had brought in preferential duties for high strength sweet Empire wines.

Worse to come, the Wall Street crash in 1929, followed by the United Kingdom going off the Gold Standard in 1931, ushered in the world depression of the early 1930s. But business in the Port trade was not as bad as it might have been, and right up to the Second World War, although the rate of consumption was static, more Port was still being drunk than any other single wine.

The *entreposto* of Vila Nova de Gaia, the twin town to Oporto on the south bank of the Douro, had been officially incorporated in 1927, and all Port stocks had to be held prior to shipment within its boundaries, or stored in the Douro region. The advent of the slump caused the Portuguese Government to set up a trade organisation in 1933, with the objects of protecting quality, controlling over-production and ensuring fair price for the farmer, all under the general control of a government-sponsored body, the Instituto do Vinho do Porto, with headquarters in Oporto, and with some modifications this organisation continues to the present time.

Economic conditions were just starting to improve when the war started in 1939. Stocks of Port in the country were drunk, or in many cases destroyed by bombing. There were some very small government-controlled shipments imported from 1942 onwards, but these hardly scratched the surface of the demand. Much more serious for the future of the trade was the terrible post-war dislocation of business caused by shortages, financial stringency, taxation and inflation, leading to further great changes in wine-drinking habits.

The Port trade was, indeed, in very low water until a slow recovery began in the early 1960s. With life more or less back to normal, and with certainly a more widespread appreciation of food and drink, the young businessman, in particular, wining and dining his friends at home and being in turn entertained by them, found a bottle of Port the ideal way to end a meal, suiting both his pocket and giving the maximum of enjoyment to guests of both sexes.

Very sensibly, the idea that the ladies must be banished to the drawing-room as soon as the Port is put on the table has been thrown out of the window, together with the old no-smoking rule. Most importantly, Port is found to be very good value for money compared with other post-prandial alternatives. I am happy to say that many restaurateurs and *sommeliers* now see that there is a decanter of Port on the liqueur trolley, and in pubs even 'Port and lemon' has been rediscovered as an acceptable long drink.

Unless prices go completely mad under inflationary pressures, or the Chancellor of the Exchequer finally kills the goose with more increases in wine duties, one can foresee a very reasonable future for 'The Englishman's Wine' in this country, and that goes for Scotsmen and Welshmen too! I think that the general quality of Port sold is higher than before the last war, while in the past few years, branded Ports bearing famous shippers' names and of first-class quality have come on the market. These wines give the British Port drinker what he has always liked, colour, body and a 'vintage style' finish on the palate.

Today there is a nostalgia for tradition and the old spacious days; what better wine than a glass or two of 'Old Oporto' to bring back those happier times.

The Douro and Viticulture

The valley of the River Douro is an unique, wild and picturesque region. Certainly no other wine-growing district gives such a breath-taking sense of majestic grandeur. The lie of the land explains why it was only opened up at the end of the seventeenth century by the intrepid English Factors who braved the greatest hardships on muleback to reach the interior. By shipping to England the wine that they had bought, they gradually achieved recognition for the Douro wines with their intense colour, body and high iron content. Such wines were better suited to the English palate and climate than the lighter, more acid and volatile wines of the Minho, a district to the north of Oporto. A protective ring of granite hills and mountains virtually surrounds the wine region and touches the Douro itself, just above the mouth of the River Tua at the Cachão da Valeira and Ferradosa, and just below the mouth of the River Sabor.

The region remains as it was originally delimited by the Marquis de Pombal between 1758 and 1761, almost the same today. It comprises about 1,250 square miles (320,000 hectares). Starting about 100 km (60 miles) as the crow flies (but certainly not as the motor-car travels) east of Oporto at Mesão Frio, it continues right to the Spanish frontier at Barca d'Alva, with the administrative capital of the whole district at Régua and the local capital of the Upper or Cima Corgo at Pinhão.

One noteworthy extension to the existing, smaller, area was made in the last quarter of the eighteenth century; the great natural eastern barrier in the course of the river, the Cachão de Valeira, was cleared over a period of several years of its larger boulders. This opened up the entire river to boats from Oporto to Barca d'Alva on the Spanish frontier. Before then the vineyards were generally planted in only the western end of the district, known as the Lower or Baixo Corgo. Viticulture has been practised there for a very long time, the vines having been introduced either by the Phoenicians, from their settlement at the mouth of the river before the first century B.C., or by the Roman legions and traders who crossed

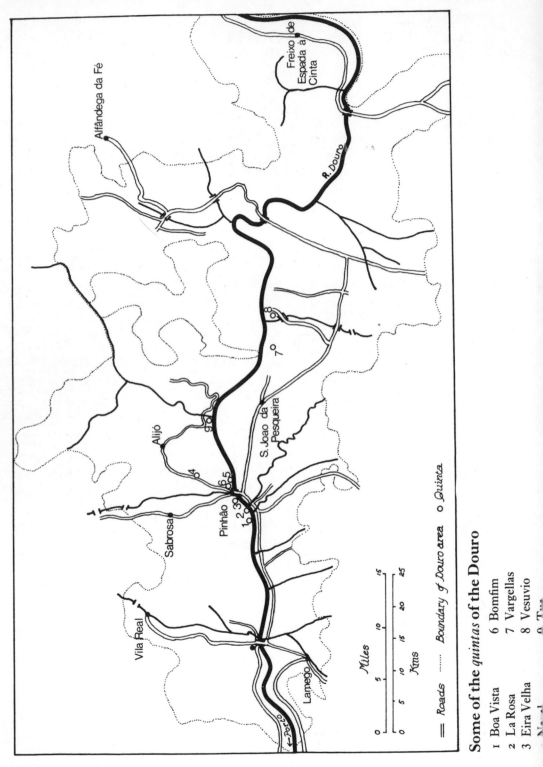

Some of the _quintas_ of the Douro

1 Boa Vista   6 Bomfim
2 La Rosa   7 Vargellas
3 Eira Velha   8 Vesuvio

Spain. The land here is less precipitous and much easier to work. Fewer of the walled terraces for planting vines, so typical of the region, had to be made laboriously by hand. From here the first Douro wines were shipped to England, and almost certainly the first fortified Port was made in this district.

Now roads link the region to Oporto, and for those who are without a car the single-line railway, which preceded the roads, can be an attractive but slow means of transport. However, it was not until after 1887 that even this single-line railway linked Oporto to Barca d'Alva on the frontier with Spain.

The principal districts which make up the region are Vila Real which includes Pinhão, Bragança, Viseu and Guarda. Of this entire area only 25,000 hectares (61,775 acres) are now under vines.

The heart of the fine wine area is around Pinhão, where some of the greatest *quintas* exist, the names of which are household words. The following are, not, of course, set out in any order of merit.

Boa Vista is famous as the backbone of Offley vintages and often shipped as a single *quinta*. Its wines are always sweet, luscious and rather scented. Sandeman's were part owners, but the *quinta* now belongs to Senhor Eulâlio José da Fonseca of Amarante and the Seminario do Christo Rei.

La Rosa, a great *quinta*, still belongs to the Feuerheerd family, and was managed for many years by Mrs. Claire Bergqvist, the daughter of Mr. Albert Feuerheerd.

Eira Velha belongs to the old West Country family of Newman and, without doubt, is one of the show places of the Douro. At the vintage the Portuguese flag, the Union Jack and the old Newman Newfoundland Shipping Line house flag, chequered blue and white, are always flown. Records show that this *quinta* was producing wine as far back as 1582, before the Newmans went to Portugal.

Noval, is, perhaps, the best known *quinta* in the whole region. Beautifully kept and laid out, it belongs to the firm of A. J. da Silva, owned by the van Zeller family. A unique feature is that some national ungrafted vines are still grown here, and though they have to be renewed periodically due to the ever-present attention of the phylloxera aphid, a few pipes of old style *nacional* Port are still made.

Roeda is Croft's premier *quinta*. Not infrequently offered by them as a single *quinta* vintage.

Bomfim, a fine property, is owned by the Symington family. Under their banner come Silva & Cosens, shipping Dow, Warre, Quarles Harris, Smith Woodhouse, and now Graham.

Vargellas, another very fine *quinta*, is owned by Taylor. Frequently offered as a single vintage.

Vesuvio was founded by the husband of the famed Dona Antonia Ferreira in the late eighteenth century. It remains in the family and is one of the largest and best tended *quintas*.

Tua belongs to Cockburn. Perhaps if I write more fully about this property I may be excused because of the deep affection I have both for the place and for those whom I have had the privilege of meeting there over the years.

In truth it must be said that until recently only a small quantity of wine was made at the *quinta*, and the house was originally bought by the firm as a convenient centre from which to control their very extensive vintage purchases in the Cima Corgo. However, in the last few years not only has the *quinta* been very greatly extended and planted for fine wine, but a controlled fermentation installation built to deal with grapes sent in by the surrounding small farmers, together with 'balloon' storage tanks for the wine produced, has been added. These tanks, made of concrete over a wire frame, are cheap to make, and excellent for keeping wine for a short time when maturing is not required.

Until fairly recently concessions to undue comfort in the house would have been considered decadent in the extreme, especially as the visits of ladies were not encouraged. The beds were like boards, there was only one bath with limited hot water, so that at vintage time when there were many guests the last to bath probably emerged dirtier than when he went in. There was only one primitive lavatory, which meant that some people had to make an early morning trip to the concealing foliage of the vineyard. But these trifling inconveniences paled to nothing in the wonderful atmosphere of good fellowship and well-being in the evening, sitting over the Port (always a special blend of old tawny drunk only in the Douro) and when there was a house-party, not infrequently ending with a sing-song culled from *The Students' Song Book*.

However, let no one who may be fortunate enough to be invited to stay at Tua be put off by this tale of possible material

barco rabelo, now rarely seen, bringing pipes of Port from the Douro. In the background the bridge of Dom Luis I
d Vila Nova de Gaia

The sharp bend at Barqueiros, the gateway to the wine area

The valley of the Douro

Tua. Cockburn's *quinta*

The old railway

Terraced vineyards

Trellising the young vines

shortcomings. There is now an abundance of comfortable beds, bathrooms, hot water and lavatories, while the wonderful atmosphere of hospitality and friendliness remains as it always has been, an oasis in a troubled world.

Even in the sixteenth century the area immediately around the city of Lamego was well established as a wine-producing region. The best wines at that time fetched a lot of money. The principal grape varieties grown today vary little from those grown three hundred years ago.

With the growth of trade, the Cima Corgo area, extending eastwards from the confluence of the River Corgo, flowing from the north, with the Douro at Régua, was cultivated with vines.

Some of the important details about the region which follow are perhaps of interest chiefly to students, such as conditions of soil and climate, grape varieties, planting, grafting and pruning, care and diseases of the vine, and flora and fauna.

Generally the soil consists of the original rock, broken up, which over the years has decomposed into a workable medium. The composition is generally schistous–sandstone, with granite predominating towards the outer boundaries of the region. Over the centuries this has become light grey in colour, shading to red, and varies in texture from clay to hard chips. The schist is the best soil for both red and white grapes and comprises the greater part of the total area, particularly along the south bank of the Douro. The granite, on the other hand, produces good whites, but poor reds. Further down the scale is a calcareous earth giving rather poorer wine and lastly the alluvial soil at the base of the valleys makes for a still coarser wine.

As with most wine regions, variations in soil within the same geographical area will cause quite extraordinary and subtle differences in the styles of the wines from the same grape.

Great extremes of climate exist. The variation in rainfall is inversely related to the average temperature. Moving upstream eastwards the temperature rises, and nearer the sea decreases. The rainfall varies widely and can reach 60 centimetres (24 inches) at Régua, half as much at Tua and half again at the Spanish frontier. The total distance is only about eighty kilometres.

In this region snow is rare, but frosts in early winter are frequent and can be severe. Happily in spring the frosts seldom cause

13

damage in the area. In the height of summer temperatures of around 40 °C (104 °F) are not uncommon and 44 °C (111 °F) has been known. There are, in fact, three micro-climates, Atlantic, Atlantic-Mediterranean and Mediterranean within the one region. The ideal is that which affects the middle reaches of the Douro and produces the finest Ports.

Below Barqueiros, where the boundary of the region lies, the Douro makes a sharp bend between two steep hills. These serve as a protective barrier against the damp Atlantic winds. A series of high mountains on the north and south banks of the Douro give further protection and also act as a shield against the cold northerly winds. This leads to climatic conditions that are peculiar to the Douro alone.

There are so many varieties of vine growing in the region, some of which are authorised, some only tolerated; the most important are those that are recommended and have proved themselves over the years to be most suitable for making the best quality wine. Among the reds are:

Tinta Francisca
Tinta Roriz
Touriga Francesa
Bastardo
Tinta Cão
Mourisco
Mourisco de Semente – a more recently introduced hybrid.
And the whites:
Malvasia Fina
Donzelinho
Moscatel Galego
Rabigato

These are but a few of the eighty-five varieties grown in the Douro, of which fifteen red and eight white are extensively used. Because of the remarkable variety of micro-climates in the region, it has been found over the centuries that this tremendous range of vines has been necessary to cope with the differences between one valley and the next. Since the infestation of the region by the phylloxera aphid in the last century, nearly all vines have had to be grafted. The American root-stocks extensively used have been *Riparia 3309*, *Monticola*, *Cordifolia*, *Aramão* and, more recently, two new hybrids of *Berlandieri*, R99 and R110 were introduced. Some of the old traditional vines used before the phylloxera did not take well on the original American stock and have now died out.

Among the many vines used for grafting today are some French varieties and some fairly recent hybrids such as *Mourisco de Semente. Mourisco, Tinta Cão* and *Touriga* date back a very long way, and happily are partially phylloxera-resistant. *Tinta Francisca*, said to be a variant of *Pinot Noir*, which has been in use for a very long time, is now less popular. One sees another variety, *Tinto Barroco*, grown extensively in the Cape winelands of South Africa, where it is called *Tintas das Baroccas*, and is the main variety used in their production of Port-style wine. Almost all, if not all, of these vines are hybrids. It is universally true of vines that the more prolific producers give the poorest quality wine. Such varieties as *Touriga* and *Tinta Cão* give the best. Production can vary according to the situation of the vines; those in the steepest and stoniest vineyards will yield as little as half a pipe per thousand vines, those on easier slopes up to six pipes, and soil variations will also play a part.

The preparation of the vineyards and the planting of the vines is more difficult in most parts of the Douro, although the advent of machinery and rising costs of labour and upkeep have led to new terraces being made on a gentle slope carrying many rows of vines. Before that, methods had changed little for over three hundred years, and cultivation is still to some extent by hand with the mattock, with the mule-drawn plough also playing a part. In the modern *quintas* the tractor can be used to good effect. However the old hands deprecate the use of the plough because of the damage it might do above or below ground level.

In the areas of the Cima Corgo producing fine wine, the slopes on which the vines had to be planted were very much steeper, so that it was necessary to build drystone walls, which sometimes retained sufficient soil to support only a single row of vines. All the work was done with iron hand-spikes and crowbars. There is an old saying, 'The wine to be good must hear the tiller'.

The soil is schist, a laminated rock which can be broken with comparative ease down to the required depth for planting, but small charges of dynamite are often used to get the work started. With the increase in the size of the vineyards, much bigger walls had to be made to hold back the earth on wider terraces, so that often huge quantities of stone had to be disposed of and incorporated in the walls. Some monumental examples of such wall-building may be seen at Tua, Boa Vista and Noval. These walls can be as much as 3 metres (9 ft 9 in) high and 1.5 metres (4 ft 10 in) thick.

Vines are planted in rows running parallel to the contours of the terraces. The normal spread allowed for each root is 1.3 × 1.10 metres (3 ft 7 in × 4 ft 4 in), but with increased mechanisation the spacing is growing. Preparation of the ground and the tilling begins soon after the vintage in readiness for the winter rains. Vines are seldom manured, there being little organic manure available in the region. Chemical fertilisers are put down during the winter, composed mainly of potassium, phosphorous and nitrogen. In established vineyards, the earth around each vine is dug over deeply in the autumn or in early winter, and any suckers are removed from the roots. This is the *escarva*. A species of lupin used to be grown between the vines and was ploughed in on flowering as a form of humus, but this practice is now rare.

The root-stocks used depend on the soil and situation of the vineyard; thus the *Berlandier; Riparia* strains 420A and SO4 are planted on the cooler lowlands and the *Rupestris* varieties E99 and R110 on the hot, dry hillsides. Grafting takes place during February and March each year. Traditionally, this has always been done *in situ*. The American vine having been planted a year earlier, the head of the year-old vine is cut off at a straight, clean spot, the stem is split and the shaped scion is inserted into the split. The stem is then bound with bass, covered with earth to keep it moist and free from damage, and left. Before being inserted each section must pass into the mouth of the grafter, who to keep his mouth properly seasoned has to have frequent recourse to a bottle of table wine, or the grafts would not take! During the last two or three years ready-grafted vines have been prepared under glass in France, the scion having been sent over from Portugal. So far the experiments have been quite small, but the results appear satisfactory and this could be an interesting development of the future. Pruning takes place from December until the end of February. Generally a form of double Guyot is employed. The two arms of the vine are left with about fourteen to sixteen buds each.

Even before grafting has taken place, props of slate or treated wood have been put up in the new vineyard to carry wires, two or three to each row at varying heights, along which the vines will be trained. The main stem of the vine is normally tied to the lowest wire, about 32 centimetres (12 inches) above the ground. When the new shoots reach the second wire, they are bent over and secured.

As in all vine-growing areas, spraying is an essential part of the year's work in a vineyard, to combat cryptogamic diseases and insect pests. Sulphur powder applications are made from April onwards to prevent *oïdium*, which first appeared in the Douro in 1857 and caused great damage. Depending upon the dampness of the season, a mixture of copper sulphate and lime is sprayed on to the vines between three and ten times a season, with an average of six. This combats the spread of mildew, which had followed the scourge of *oïdium*, appearing in 1893 in the Douro.

From March to May it may be necessary to plough or hoe out the weeds at intervals – today they may be treated with herbicides. In July, depending on the situation of the vineyard and the weather, some of the vine leaves will be removed to increase the ripening of the grapes.

Other worries the Douro farmer may face during the season are such pests and diseases as *altica ampelophaga*, which occurs in very wet years. If the vine is sprayed with an organic pesticide at the time of the first application of Bordeaux mixture, the insect will be destroyed before it lays its eggs on the underside of the leaves. The grape-moth, which includes *cochylis* and *eudemis*, has also appeared in recent years in the Douro. Usually, two sprayings with a phosphoric compound will prevent the eggs from hatching, but if allowed to go unchecked the larvae will eat young grapes and the affected bunches will rot. In about 1948 a disease called *maromba* reappeared in the Douro. It had been noted as far back as 1845 and wrongly diagnosed as a virus. However, it is, in fact, due to a deficiency of boron in the soil, and by the application of borax to the ground, according to the level of acidity in the soil, the yield of grapes per hectare is markedly increased.

From August onwards there is little or nothing to do in the vineyards until the vintage, which usually starts about the middle of September and lasts for three to four weeks. The viticultural cycle ends with the vintage, which is as colourful in the Douro area as in many other wine-making districts – perhaps even more so. Production varies from 600–700 pipes (950 kilos of grapes per pipe) on the biggest *quintas* in the Baixo Corgo, down to two or three baskets of grapes (70 kilos per basket) in the thousands of small holdings in the Cima Corgo. In between these two extremes are a number of *quintas* producing from 100–250 pipes, many of 20–80, and hundreds from 1–15 pipes. Very few medium and smaller farms now make their own wine on their premises, the grapes are bought by the big farmers, shippers or the government-sponsored co-operatives.

Due to the almost total stoppage of shipments during the last war, many new regulations regarding grafting, planting and the amount of Port each property can make came into force. A points system was devised taking all relevant factors into account and for ease of reference this is set out as an Appendix (*see page 109*).

The region of production abounds in a variety of wild flowers, insects and birds. In the spring and early summer there is a wealth of colourful flowers on the hillsides and in the valleys; white and yellow broom, lavender, honeysuckle, gorse, dog-rose, mimosa, poppy, viper's bugloss, vetch, foxglove, flax, harebell, cornflower, lupin, mallow, antirrhinum, iris, jonquil, daffodil, grape hyacinth, heart's-ease, saxifrage and stonecrop, to name a few. Along the river bank are alders, willows and tamarisk. On the higher ground are evergreen oak, juniper, gum cistus in varying colours of yellow, mauve and white, wild olive, chestnut, wild pear, cork, fig, and overall a variety of lichens. The scents are wonderful and the scenery spectacular.

Despite its sometimes forbidding face the region is a home for many beautiful birds, animals and insects. With this mass of plant life on which to feed, the insect population is very large and attracts in its turn birds and animals. Almost all the commoner European species of butterflies breed freely, including the painted lady, camberwell beauty, red admiral, large and small tortoiseshell, Queen of Spain fritillary, clouded yellow, various skippers, meadow browns, yellow brimstone, orange tip, ringlets, long- and short-tailed blues and purple emperor. Some very beautiful moths such as the death's-head hawk moth are common.

Less attractive, perhaps, but of interest to naturalists are the other forms of insect life, including crickets, grasshoppers, occasionally locusts, scorpions, giant armoured centipedes, praying mantis, various species of ant, bees, wasps, ichneumon fly, and, some years ago, the malarial mosquito. There are, however, many attractive and more harmless insects, especially in the evening.

When the fireflies and the glow-worms are out there is a great sense of peace.

Although there are resident birds, the area is most lively when the spring and autumn bring the migrating visitors; green and golden plover, snipe, woodcock, little grebe, and varieties of duck. If the weather is bad out at sea, gulls and terns appear, and Pallas's sand-grouse have been known to weather storms inland.

Resident birds include the commoner birds seen in the British Isles, and in addition in the Upper Douro are seen the Egyptian vulture, the eagle owl, and along the river, the dipper, the rare blue rock thrush, kingfisher, black redstart, heron, black kite, kestrel, black wheatear and the azure-winged magpie. In the western end of the region a few golden eagles still live and in the olive trees around Pinhão the shy golden oriole can be seen darting through the leaves.

The fish life on the river has of course been greatly affected by the construction of dams, and the chad and lampreys that travelled upstream are no longer seen. There are still rudd, carp and crayfish, but trout are rare and the occasional sturgeon can no longer pass the dam.

Some of the animals of the region are now rare and not often seen in other parts of Europe. In the Marão mountains and close to the frontier the occasional wolf and wild boar can be found, while others, seldom seen, are the marten, the lynx and the wild cat. Commoner are the fox, badger, weasel, brown rat, hedgehog, hare, rabbit and several types of bat, of which the little pipistrelle is quite common.

To this wealth of living things, should be added the water tortoise, gecko lizards, the giant blue lizard, which is especially beautiful, various toads and frogs, the grass snake, smooth snake and adder.

To return to the river itself, where possible irrigation has been tried, but insufficient study has been made of the subject so far. With the change in the river levels caused by the recently-built dams, it is possible that more irrigation will be used in future.

Though some old Douro hands may disagree, I think the extra expanses of water enhance the beauty of the countryside. It is still too early to know the effect of the new water levels on climate and on wine production, although government-inspired studies have been inaugurated.

What the dams should do is prevent the floods which have been a feature of the river in the past, sometimes disastrous, even sweeping ships out to sea and wrecking them on the bar of the Douro. At Cockburn's most up-country *quinta*, Cadima, there are six marks on the wall showing the great *cheias* (floods) of December 1909, February 1936, January 1940, March 1947, February 1960 and January 1962. Looking at the placid river it seems quite incredible that it could rise so high. Certainly in the last flood, casks of Port floated out through the roof of the lodge and were eventually found unharmed under the nearby railway bridge spanning the river.

Before modern roads were built, the only methods of transport in the Douro were by boat on the river, locally on foot or horseback and, for long distances, the train, the wonderfully engineered single-line right to the Spanish frontier. Modern diesel loc-omotives have now made their appearance, and their melodious hooting echoing round the hills is very much part of the character of the Douro. From Tua there is a delightful narrow-gauge line running north to Mirandela; the tank engines are mostly French dating from the 1880s, real museum pieces, but still beautifully maintained. I think one of the most intriguing sights I have seen was at Pinhão station during the 1975 vintage, when we were suddenly aware of a large party of Japanese train-spotters, all suitably armed with cameras and note-books.

The roads, though hair-raising in the mountains, are excellently metalled, and with the general use of cars the necessity of getting on a horse to visit remote *quintas* is now a rare occurrence. For one who is no horseman this is a blessing, especially as, on the last occasion I had to ride. I had quite a narrow squeak. During the very hot vintage of 1948, on a visit to an outlying *quinta*, I was riding an animal which had box-stirrups, not uncommon in these parts. Having with some difficulty got my feet firmly wedged in these contraptions, we eventually reached the sandy bank of the river preparatory to being picked up by boat. I was suddenly conscious of an indescribable sensation and realised that the horse, which was probably even hotter than I was, was keeling over and was about to roll with my feet firmly jammed. With a last despairing heave, just as it was capsizing, I got my feet free.

Many visitors to the Douro will remember exciting excursions on the river by boat and my wife recalls the following:

'The boat trip at vintage time is the highlight of a wonderful and interesting holiday. The Douro boatmen row standing up, Venetian-style. The long sweep of their oars needs the help of the current to make good progress, so generally they come up river the evening before and meet us at Cadima.

We walk down to the sandy edge of the river and are helped on board by the crew. Hampers of *bolinhos* (fish cakes) and cold meats and round wooden *cantils* (small containers) of Port are also loaded to sustain us during the day. The boat is pushed off and down river we go, one man steering with his oar at the stern and the others standing and pushing on their oars in the prow.The scene is peaceful, the river runs lazily and the sun gets warmer as the day goes on so that by midday it is really hot. On either side the hills, with their terraces of vines, olives and almonds, rise up steeply. The single-line railway runs along the edge of the river, an alternative method of visiting the *quintas*. The mountains are brown and the greenery is provided by the olives and almonds, as by now the vine leaves are turning reddish-brown. One can still hear the bullock-carts squeaking round the tracks on the *quintas*, and see rows of pickers making their way to the lodges with baskets on their heads, or perhaps with mules or donkeys laden with baskets of grapes on either side.

The boatmen find a sandy cove for us to land at the first *quinta* we are to visit and we scramble ashore. Frequently I have looked up at the *quinta* from below and wondered how I would ever walk up what appeared to be a perpendicular track. The regulars do it with ease but I arrive purple in the face, puffing hard, though at least I get there.

The wine is tested for sugar content, the fermentation in the *lagars* is inspected and so are the empty vats into which the wine will be stored. This is an interesting performance – the small oval door in the front is opened, (for some reason it is always sealed with newspaper), you bang your hand on the vat and stick your head in the hole. The aroma that greets you is very potent, and if one kept one's head in for long I feel one would go into a peaceful coma.

The farmer then asks us to taste his special brand of Port, and we generally meet his family. Having been revived by this excellent Port we can slither downhill back to the boat quite quickly. Two or three *quintas* are generally visited in the morning, then we pull into the bank for lunch, which is always delicious and helped by more Port, and takes quite a long time. More *quintas* are visited in the afternoon, then as evening comes, we wrap our jerseys round us and the boatmen row us down to Tua, perhaps crossing rapids which to them are no problem. Part of the journey is through the Cachão gorge where Baron Forrester lost his life. Forbidding rocks rise sheer on either side. It can be a gloomy spot.

Now the boat trip has gone to make way for progress. The river trip is a thing of the past, to be remembered with pleasure by those lucky enough to have travelled that way.'

Like all farmers, the Douro farmer is extremely hospitable, and although mechanisation and the modern time factor have reduced the scale and frequency of his hospitality, a meal in his house is a pleasure not to be missed if opportunity offers. When I first knew the Douro it was no unusual thing, before lunch, for a litter of piglets to be ushered into the living-room; one would pick one's fancy, and sucking-pig would be served in due course. Such extreme forms of gastronomic selection may no longer be practised, but the guest will certainly be given a welcome to remember.

It should be a source of modest pride that still the most binding oath of the older farmer is not sworn on the Bible but 'on the word of an Englishman'.

Port Production

Until the early 1950s and the advent of the first modern wineries in the Douro, Port wine-making had changed very little over the past 150 years. Traditionally the wine was made in the following manner.

After picking, the grapes were tipped into a shallow stone trough or *lagar* which would hold between 2,250–15,900 litres (500–3,500 gallons). The grapes were crushed by foot or by simple roller crushers, and fermentation usually started within twenty-four hours. During fermentation in vats, colour extraction in the case of red wines, was obtained by regular treading or punching down, so that the skins of the grapes were kept always in close contact with the must. This regular movement also prevented the pomace from becoming a breeding ground for acid-producing bacteria.

Fermentation in the *lagars* was allowed to continue until the must contained 4°–6° alcohol (Gay-Lussac (GL)), after which the must was run off and fortified with grape brandy at 77° (GL). The pomace was then pressed either by simple vertical basket presses, or still, in some cases, by more primitive wooden presses. The pressings in the case of red wines, which were rich in colour and tannin, were then recombined with the already fortified must, or fortified and kept separate as dry wine for blending. As the concentration of alcohol after fortification is between 17°–19° GL, and the specific gravity of the wine between 1,015–1,030, the natural fermentation slows down and finally stops within twenty-four to forty-eight hours, or in some years it may take longer.

Although the traditional *lagar* is still used to make a considerable percentage of Port, modern wineries have existed in the Douro for the last twenty years. They are owned either by shippers, individual farmers or farmers' co-operatives and, if properly run, provide wine-making facilities where grapes can be transformed into wine under hygienic conditions with the minimum involvement of labour.

Before discussing modern methods of vinification, one should examine the design of a modern winery.

Owing to the geography of the Douro region and its poor communications, in order to avoid undue delays between picking and crushing, small wineries are distributed over the region as a whole, ranging in capacity from about 500 to 10,000 pipes.

Nowadays, the majority of grapes are transported by road to the winery in mild-steel resin-painted containers holding approximately 1,000 kg (2,200 lb) of grapes, or in traditional wickerwork baskets. Weighing is normally performed by a weighbridge, and samples of grape must will be taken for density analysis to determine roughly how much fermentable sugar the grapes contain. Automatic recording refractometers are available in the more modern wineries for this purpose.

After weighing, the containers are lifted off the lorries, and the grapes are discharged into open concrete tanks with sloping sides. A continuous Archimedes screw then transports the grapes to the crushers. Although there are still some roller crushers at wineries, the tendency is to use centrifugal crushers which will automatically remove either part or all of the stalks. Sulphur dioxide is added to the grapes, either before crushing in the form of sodium metabisulphite, or after in the form of a solution of the gas in water. After the crushing, the grapes are transported to the fermentation area by means of a large bore piston-pump, connected to a permanent pipeline system, normally of plastic.

Fermentation tanks are constructed of concrete, resin-painted concrete, resin-painted mild steel or of stainless steel, of capacity normally ranging from 10 pipes to 45 pipes. This is equivalent to about 5,040–22,680 litres (1,120–5,040 gallons).

In the main, two types of fermentation tank now exist, the open-tank system and the closed-tank, the latter developed from the Algerian autovinification system.

The open-tank system is open to the atmosphere, and to achieve colour extraction during fermentation, must is withdrawn from the bottom valve and is pumped up to the top of the tank, where it is sprayed over the grape skins.

In the closed system the pressure exerted by carbon dioxide gas, the main by-product of fermentation, is used as a means of motive power to withdraw must from the fermentation tank and to cascade it back down over the grape skins. The closed system is automatic only when fermentation has started, whereas the open system does allow pumping over at any time before or during fermentation and is not dependant on the pressure developed by large quantities of carbon dioxide.

The more modern fermentation tanks are fitted with a conical bottom so that when the fermentation has produced the required amount of natural alcohol, the must will be run off and fortified. The pomace which remains, and which accounts for between 20–25% of the volume, can be discharged by simply opening a large manhole situated in the bottom of the tank. This obviates the necessity of emptying the tanks by hand, which is both a dangerous and a time-consuming operation.

The pomace is either discharged into a dejuicer, which gives a light pressing, and then into a basket or other type of press, or, in more automated wineries, falls into another cement trough with a continuous screw in the bottom, which then transports the pomace to the pressing section. For reasons of hygiene this section is usually separate from the rest of the winery.

It is normal practice here in the pressing section to pass the pomace through a dejuicer, before it is processed by continuous or Vaslin-type presses.

Yield of must from the pomace after fermentation varies, but in an average year, 60–70% of the total is free-run from the pomace simply by gravity, 15–20% is expressed by the dejuicer and 5–15% by the final pressing.

The continuous press tends to be more favoured in modern wineries. It is simple to operate and, once set up, requires little or no attention during the vintage. Yield of pressed juice is high, and in most models pressings can be separated into two or three fractions, according to tannin content and astringency.

The length of fermentation is short; hence the period of colour extraction is limited, therefore efficient pressing is very important if maximum colour yield is to be obtained. Unlike production of red table wines, where the pressings are often kept separate and used for distilling material, the colour and body of red Port depends to some extent on the inclusion of these pressings in the finished wine.

White Port can be made either by fermentation with the skins, or by the fermentation of free-run juice without the skins. Free-run juice can be produced by holding crushed grapes in tank until natural draining produces enough must, or by the use of pro-prietary dejuicers linked to a continuous Vaslin or basket press.

Better quality musts are probably produced by holding crushed grapes in a draining tank, as they are exposed to much less physical maceration than they would be if dejuiced by mechanical means.

White Port produced from free-run juice results in a rather neutral wine, devoid of many of the intrinsic characteristics of the grape, whereas fermentation in the presence of skins does give the wine more flavour and vinous characteristics.

After pressing, the pomace is sold or stored in silos until after the vintage, when it is steam distilled to produce a fiery spirit called *bagaçeira*. Finally the remains are used as vineyard manure, and the pips for chicken food.

At present no recovery of tartaric acid or colouring pigment from the pomace is attempted in the Douro region.

Fermentation of sugar results in the liberation of large quantities of heat. In small containers most of this heat is lost by radiation, but in fermentation tanks part of this heat is retained and as a consequence the temperature raised. High fermentation temperatures of $36°-38°C (97°-100°F)$ results in the wine yeast losing its fermentative abilities, and loss of flavour and aroma in the finished wine. Apart from damage to the flavour of the wine, high fermentation temperatures lead to the growth of heat resistant spoilage bacteria, and unless sufficient levels of sulphur dioxide are maintained in the must, acidification will take place with the consequent production of large quantities of acetic acid (vinegar) and ethyl acetate.

The more sophisticated Douro wineries have refrigeration equipment to control the fermentation temperatures, and it is generally considered that for red wines fermentation temperatures should be between $26°-27°C, (79°-81°F)$ and for white wines two or three degrees lower. Refrigeration equipment normally consists of small compressors which chill water down to $0°-5°C, (32°-41°F)$. This water is then circulated against wine in tubular heat exhangers, or circulated in cooling coils or heat exchangers actually within the fermentation vat.

Little or no use of yeast starters (addition of dried or fermenting yeast of known strains) is made to promote rapid fermentation, reliance being put on the wild yeasts which are present in the winery.

It can be calculated that wine made in the traditional *lagar* took about twenty man-hours per pipe, whereas in a modern winery this period can be reduced to approximately thirty man-minutes per pipe.

Wine-making

In an average year, 750 kg (1,650 lb) of grapes yield approximately 550 litres (120 gallons) of must, and if 450 litres (100 gallons) of fermented must, which contains $4°-6°$ GL alcohol, are mixed with 100 litres (22 gallons) of brandy at $77°$ GL, the resulting wine will have an alcohol content of approximately $17°-19°$ GL.

As grapes are received at the winery they are visually examined to ensure that they are free from mould, bruising, leaves and other debris. A sample of grapes is crushed, and the juice is examined by a refractometer or weighed with a hydrometer to ascertain the *baumé* or specific gravity, which is normally between 11–13 or 1.083–1.100 in gravity. From these readings the wine-maker can judge the maturity of the grapes, and have an approximation of the degree of alcohol these grapes will contribute after fermentation. Obviously the sweeter the grape the less brandy has to be added on fortification.

Centrifugal crushers will remove automatically a variable percentage of stalks. The percentage removed depends on the wine-maker but the following applies:

(1) A percentage of stalks helps to improve the handling and draining of both unfermented and fermented pomace.

(2) Absence of stalks leads to higher fermentation temperatures.

(3) Quality of white wines may be adversely affected by the inclusion of too many stalks, especially during pressing.

Immediately before or after crushing, sulphur dioxide is added to the must. Very little is needed when the grapes are in perfect condition and cool; in practice 100–200 mg per litre is used.

Apart from effective antiseptic action against spoilage bacteria, wines made from sulphur dioxide-treated musts normally have, in the case of reds, a deeper colour, and for both red and white, lower volatile acidity and higher extract in comparison with wines made from non-sulphited musts.

Once the fermentation tank is full, with the open tank, the must is pumped out of the bottom and sprayed over the pomace at intervals to keep the skins and solid matter fresh and moist, to prevent ingress of flies and acetification. In the case of the Algerian closed tank there is very little to do except wait until fermentation starts. The various acetic bacteria transform alcohol in the presence of oxygen into vinegar, or acetic acid and water. If the grapes were received under hot conditions some cooling may be used, if available, to reduce the temperature of the must to 25 °C (77 °F).

Normally within twenty-four hours fermentation starts, and the wine-maker follows its course by taking gravity readings with a hydrometer. Only when fermentation starts does the extraction of colour become noticeable. This is because the alcohol produced tends to increase the release of the colouring pigments, which are trapped in the cells of the grape skins.

Due to the heat of fermentation, temperatures can rise rapidly; hence, if cooling is available every effort is made to keep the temperature down to below 28 °C (82 °F).

During fermentation, must in open tanks is pumped over frequently to encourage good colour extraction and to keep the skins free from acetifying bacteria. In the closed tank, the frequency of must withdrawal and its re-entry over the pomace can be controlled with a simple pressure valve. Ideally this occurs every twenty to thirty minutes during the height of fermentation. *(See diagram in Appendix p. 116)*

Fermentation is continued under normal conditions for about thirty-six hours, by which time the *baumé* will have dropped from, for example, 12° down to the level required by the wine-maker; this depends on the degree of residual sweetness wanted in the final wine, but most normal wines are run off between 6°–7°. The fermenting must is run off into a vat together with the required amount of brandy, normally 450 litres (100 gallons) must to 100 litres (22 gallons) brandy. Pressings from the pomace are added, and the contents thoroughly mixed to ensure that the brandy is not, because of its low density, floating on the must. If this occurs, fermentation continues and the residual sugar is lost.

White wine can be made in a similar manner except that if fermented with the skins less pumping over is needed as no colour extraction is required.

Sweet wines, which contain virtually all the grape sugar, are made by fermenting the must with the skins for very little time, so that there is hardly a drop in density. These are, in the case of red wines, naturally light in colour and are fortified with up to 150 litres (33 gallons) brandy to 400 litres (88 gallons) must.

Some varieties of Port grapes

Another variety

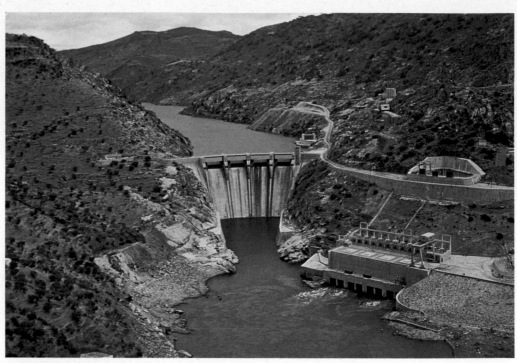

The new dam in the Douro

View of the Douro

The grape pickers

The grapes are carried to the *quinta*

The grapes arrive at the *quinta*

After the vintage, wines receive their first racking either in November or the spring, the lees are removed and the wine is brought up to 18.5° (GL) with the addition of more brandy. Depending on the system of vinification used and the year, the first lees represent an average between 5–9% of the total volume.

Racking as soon after the vintage as possible is to be recommended, as early removal of yeast prevents loss of colour, which occurs when the colouring matter is absorbed into the yeast cell wall, and the release into the wine from the break-down of dead yeast of vitamins and growth factors which will stimulate the growth of spoilage bacteria. Regular racking and addition of brandy during the first year is an important contribution to ensuring that the wine remains free of infection by acid-producing micro-organisms. The number of rackings a wine receives during its maturation very much depends on the ideas of the individual wine-maker. In some houses wines are racked every three months in the first year, twice in the second and less frequently as the wine ages.

Brandy

Brandies for fortification are selected by tasting and smell, and those with a clean but aromatic character are preferred.

Final operation

Final clarification of Port is achieved essentially through filtration, fining or refrigeration, or a combination of the three processes.

White wines

Owing to maturation for long periods in wood, white wines gain a considerable amount of colour, which has to be removed before the wine is shipped. Excess colour can be removed by the addition of gelatin together with tannin, or the use of milk, isinglass and casein.

After fining, a further treatment with bentonite is sometimes used, to finally remove proteins, which have either been introduced by the fining agents themselves or which have not been removed by their action.

To prevent the precipitation of the potassium and calcium salts of tartaric acid, refrigeration is the only suitable method currently available. Wine is chilled to within 2° of its freezing point and held at this temperature for sufficient time to allow precipitation of the tartrates. After tartrate deposition is achieved, the wine is either pad or Kieselguhr-filtered. In some chilling systems no holding period at low temperature is used. The wine, however, is held briefly in a vessel which is designed to precipitate the tartrates.

In the case of white wines the refrigeration does little to remove colour, and complete stability of a wine can only be obtained by the use of fining and cold treatment.

Red wines

Fining has been the traditional method of clarification of red wines for generations. The agent most used is gelatin; generally no extra tannin has to be added. The fining tends to remove from the wine a certain amount of colour and tannin, which tends to make the wine softer and give it slightly more age. Hence it is a useful tool in the hands of the wine-maker. Although fining procedures result in clarification, if wine then is bottled, especially young or dark wine, it will after a time throw a further deposit in the bottle. Although this is acceptable for crusting Ports, etc., the customer for ruby and tawny requires the wine to be poured bright to the last drop.

Refrigeration of red wines down to within 2°C of their freezing point results in the precipitation of unstable colouring matter, which is responsible for the clouding of wine after bottling. The wine is normally held for sufficient time at this temperature to allow precipitation to occur, and then cold filtered through a pad or Kieselguhr filter at the same temperature. The addition of small quantities of an antioxidant such as sulphur dioxide at this stage, when the wine is still cold, preferably before filtration, protects the wine against air, which could cause further instability. Careful use of refrigeration, followed by employment of sulphur dioxide and storage in full tanks before bottling with minimum aeration, can give a young ruby wine a considerable shelf life. This is to say that under normal conditions no further clouding or throwing of a deposit should occur during this time. The quality and essential taste of the wine is not of course, impaired by these deposits, but to the uninitiated, the look of a 'cloudy' bottle might cause misgivings.

Filtration

As Port has a high alcohol content, normally there is little need to subject the wine to a sterilising filtration. Filtration is used finally to polish the wine after fining or refrigeration, or in the case of lees, to recover Port from solid material.

Both Kieselguhr and pad filters are used for these operations, Kieselguhr filters being especially useful for handling larger quantities.

Vintage Port

We have seen how and why 'Red Portugal' or Port became a known and accepted wine in England, even though in the early days of the trade it had sometimes been strongly criticised on the score of quality, particularly by disappointed seekers after claret.

It required two discoveries, however, to make Vintage Port, and indeed all Port, into the wine we know today. Firstly, the addition of wine alcohol to the fermenting must, thus retaining the sugar, which was introduced at the start of the nineteenth century, secondly the evolution of the modern cylindrical bottle, which could be binned away securely on its side, and in which maturation could take place without disturbance. The secret of maturing wine in earthenware or glass containers had been lost to Europe since the Falernian, so appreciated by Horace. The debt owed to Vintage Port, for reviving the possibilities of ageing in bottle for fine and long-lived wine, particularly by claret, is immense and enduring.

Very fortunately, the turn of the eighteenth and beginning of the nineteenth centuries coincided with a series of remarkably fine Vintages, culminating in the 'Waterloo' of 1815. Furthermore the presence of Wellington's army in Portugal brought to the attention of the right people at the right time just how good Vintage Port could be. From this time, Vintage Port became the standard-bearer for the whole Port trade, on which its prestige and reputation was built and enhanced.

What is Vintage Port? To summarise, the Portuguese Wine Laws on the subject approved by the Instituto do Vinho do Porto on 24 November 1970, and revised as from 1 January 1974, state:–

Vintage, Two to Three Year Bottling

(1) Samples must be submitted by the shipper to the Instituto do Vinho do Porto between 1 January and 30 September of the second year.

(2) The wine shall be offered *in Bottle only* under the *Selo de Guarantia* (Seal of Guarantee), and should be bottled between 1 July of the second year and 30 June of the third year.

A Vintage is usually 'declared' to the trade in the spring of the second year after the harvest, and will be offered to the public that autumn when the wine is actually bottled.

In the Appendix is a list of Vintages by the best-known shippers since 1870. It is impossible to achieve complete accuracy and omissions may be found. The list should be regarded therefore only as a general guide.

Late Bottled Vintage (L.B.V.)

In general the same rules apply, but the year of bottling must be between 1 July of the fourth year and 31 December of the sixth year after the proposed vintage. The year of bottling must appear on the label. This style of Vintage has achieved considerable popularity of recent years, particularly in the restaurant trade. Having had a minimum of nearly four years ageing in cask, it can be handled as a Wood Port and should need no decanting. But a word of warning for the unwary, who may order a glass of 'Vintage' in a hotel or a restaurant, expecting a conventional two-year bottled wine and may be served with L.B.V. without comment. Because of its age in wood, it is much lighter in colour and body and without the distinctive 'nose' and flavour given by bottle age. In general, shippers do not offer as L.B.V. the same year that they declare their *crème de la crème* for two-year bottling. L.B.V.s therefore, are usually of good, if not supreme quality.

Crusted Port

Though not a Vintage, Crusted Port has one attribute in common with two-year bottlings, that of maturing in bottle. Crusted Port is normally a young blended wine and can therefore be 'followed' like any other of the shipper's 'marks'. Moreover, the blend can be made up so that the wine comes round in bottle ready to drink in as little as three years. These wines are not of the superb quality of Vintage, and being quicker maturing are reasonably priced. They should be handled and decanted in the same way as Vintage, and on the right occasion make a very acceptable substitute. 'Crusting Port' (my own definition) is Crusted Port freshly bottled before it is ready to drink.

Port with date of Vintage

Again the basic rules apply, but the selected wine must be at least seven years old. The label must show the vintage year, an indication that the wine has been aged in wood, and the date of bottling. Although found in many other countries, this type of wine does not have a great following in Britain.

Sometimes bottles which bear on the label the word *garrafeira* will appear in the saleroom or may more often be seen in Portugal. It is difficult to translate *garrafeira* directly into English. Usually it refers to the wine of a Portuguese shipper or farmer of his own cellar, rather like the cabinet wine of a German wine-grower. The wine is of a Vintage, but very often consecutive years will be bottled without regard to generally 'declared' Vintages. Traditionally the bottles are binned vertically and mature probably more quickly. Certainly the corks are replaced with new ones at regular intervals.

So far as this country is concerned, although Late Bottled Vintage has gained quite a following over the last few years, what we generally mean by Vintage Port, on which the foundations of the trade rest, is the British convention of wine usually bottled after two years and matured in bottle till ready to drink. But outside the United Kingdom, with the exception of a small quantity in Denmark, Scandinavia and Holland, 'English Vintage' is very rarely met with, though shop windows in Germany, Switzerland and Belgium frequently give considerable prominence to L.B.V. and 'Port with a date'. In the United States all three types of Vintage are met with, to the consequent bewilderment of Americans. We must, therefore, be prepared sometimes to shed our former Imperial and insular certainties on Vintage Port when talking with our E.E.C. colleagues or American friends, and be quite sure that the basis of the discussion refers to the same sort of Vintage.

The wine is of a year selected by the shipper as being outstanding. It is usually a blend from several *quintas*, sometimes owned by a shipper of the wine or by various farmers, in a relationship often going back for generations. Some shippers do have exceptionally fine and large *quintas* which are the backbone of their Vintage 'lot', and these are sometimes 'declared' by themselves; Taylor's Vargellas is one case in point, while Noval is always offered as a single *quinta* by the shippers.

The size of each shipper's 'lot' varies considerably, depending on the yield of the particular year and on the likely demand from the trade. The shipper must also assess the size of his 'lot', against his requirements for fine Wood Ports, particularly the very high quality Vintage Character Brands, that are now a feature of the market.

Although automation now plays such a big part in wine-making in the Douro, I am sure I can speak for some firms, and certainly for Cockburn's, in saying that the wines for a Vintage lot are still almost entirely made in the traditional way by treading in the *lagar*.

Bottling

When I started in the trade in 1930 before the giant post-war amalgamations got under way, there were hundreds of wine merchants, some of them very small, and many independent brewers, most of whom were potential customers for Vintage from more than one shipper. The wine would be imported in bulk from about the middle of the second year, and bottled traditionally 'on a nice bright autumn day'. Many bottlers had their own tricks of the trade in how they actually handled their wines. Eastern Counties' bottlings were usually considered to be amongst the best, Irish were well thought of, but I was taught that Scottish bottlings could be suspect as they might use old whisky bottles without punts. Perhaps the Scots traditional allegiance to claret was the real trouble, hence the old jingle at the time of the Act of Union:

> *Firm and erect the Caledonian stood*
> *Old was his Mutton and his Claret good*
> *'Drink Port' the English statesman cried,*
> *He drank the poison and his spirit died.*

I remember an experiment in bottling methods which Cockburn made with the 1960 vintage. It had always been the practice to allow Vintage Port to fall bright, and then to bottle unfined and, of course, unfiltered when the wine was ready. After discussing other techniques used by some of our customers, we set aside some pipes of the 1960 to bottle in three different ways. Firstly, our traditional method of allowing the wine to fall bright; this would take three to four weeks, whilst the cask rested undisturbed, and particles in suspension in the wine settled as lees in the bottom of the cask; secondly, rolling the cask up and down the cellar so that it never rested and, thirdly, allowing the wine to fall bright, then rolling and immediately bottling lees and all. Then at six monthly intervals we tasted the three bottlings blind, often asking customers and competitors to join us. The average result was always the same, the third method, bottling after the wine had fallen bright and then rolling, came out top. We therefore, bottled the 1963 and subsequent vintages in this way. Why this method, which seems on the face of it quite illogical, should come out the best, I am unable to explain. These curiosities are one of the many joys in a modern and now largely mechanised wine trade.

The cork is of prime importance in a bottle of Vintage Port in view of the time it may have to remain 'wine-proof'. 'Full-long' corks of the highest quality from Portugal's own cork forests are used, branded with the name of the shipper, the year and sometimes the date of bottling. In the old days the name of the bottler was also sometimes branded. The top of the cork and bottle is sealed with a capsule; lead being still the best material, though sometimes the old-fashioned melted wax is used. This seal finishes the job, but, more important, protects the cork against the risk of cork weevil, though this is minimal in modern storage conditions.

Storage temperature should be about 13°–16° C, but consistency of temperature is much more important than the exact degree. The wine should be stored with the label, or in the case of old Port of pre-Labelling Act days, with the white splash at the bottom of the bottle uppermost. The crust will then form on the underside of the bottle. A storage curiosity is that Portuguese Port shippers and private cellar owners usually bin their Port standing up and they seem to come to no harm. The wines are mostly L.B.V.s and wines with date of vintage.

In the old days 'shotted' bottles, pitted with shot from a cartridge shaken up by hand, were often used, and the crust was said to adhere more firmly to the uneven surface, but such refinements are now prohibitively expensive.

Decanting

A lot of unnecessary mystery is woven round the question of decanting. The bottle to be decanted should be stood up for 24–48 hours, or as long as possible beforehand, so that all loose pieces of crust will fall to the bottom. The cork, unless the wine is very old, should draw without too much difficulty; the problem these days being to find a really long corkscrew with a good thread. With a steady hand and the label or splash on the upper surface of the bottle, pour the wine into a suitable receptacle, such as a water jug, taking care not to set up a surge. Stop decanting as soon as bits of loose crust begin to appear in the neck. It will help to have a fairly strong light on the other side of the bottle; the light will shine through the wine during decanting. It may be prudent, particularly if there is the risk of an old cork crumbling, to decant through a clean piece of muslin or a handkerchief. In any case, any 'floaters' in the jug can be extracted before the wine is poured into the decanter. Before using, rinse both jug and decanter with a drop of Wood Port, to be sure they are quite clean and smell nice.

There is a trick, peculiar so far as I know to Cockburn's, in knocking off the neck of a bottle if the cork is too tight to draw or is very old and crumbly. Take off the capsule and insert the corkscrew in the normal way as far as it will go. Put the bottle on a table, for safety's sake with a cloth round it, and hold it firmly. Then, using a fairly heavy object with a flat edge, such as an old-fashioned carving knife (or better still a cold chisel), hit upwards quite gently and with a loose wrist against the flange. If all goes well, the neck of the bottle will crack quite cleanly about half-way between the top of the neck and the shoulder, and with the cracked piece still held firmly in place by the lower third or so of the cork. Draw this small remnant of cork with the corkscrew already positioned, and it should come out quite easily, then decant in the ordinary way.

On the subject of decanting and decanters, it is worth knowing that, with ships' decanters, the ratio of the measurement of the circumference of the lip to the vertical height from the lip to the base is constant and is, in fact, for some inexplicable reason, the same, or at any rate approximately so. Modest wagers can be won on this after dinner.

Serving

A question frequently asked is when Vintage Port should be opened. There are divergent views on this, but personally I am a convinced early opener, and am sure that far more bottles fail to show up as well as they should because of too late rather than too early decanting. For a wine with some youth, I would decant many hours before use, sometimes the previous day, and even for an old Vintage, two hours or so before drinking, leaving the stopper of the decanter out.

The time a wine will last once decanted, before becoming flat and uninteresting, is again a question of age. A young Port will last several days, an old one perhaps only a day or two, the common denominator being the air space in the decanter; the more air, the less time it will remain really enjoyable for drinking.

How long will Vintage Port last in bottle? I was often asked this question on the telephone by members of the public and my reply was always the same, 'Sir (or Madam), unless you are a babe in arms it will see you out'. This is so, because with the 25% or so of wine alcohol in the wine, it will never become vinegar. In extreme old age it will have lost nearly all its colour, be spirity and not very attractive, but it will be drinkable.

I can quote two examples of this. In 1965 Cockburn celebrated its 150th anniversary, and we had just one magnum of 1851 for the top table, the rest having to make do with something a little younger. I had the privilege of sitting next to André Simon, then, I think, in his early eighties. The '51, thought to be light and dry, was still fruity, flavoury and quite delicious, all and more than could be expected from a pre-phylloxera magnum. 'Ah' said A.L.S., 'I remember this when it was in its prime.' Stupidly, I did not ask him when this was, but even allowing for old age it must have been the late 1890s.

The other example arose from the good fortune that in 1939, an old Essex wine merchant, Gardner of Little Coggeshall, left in his will five or six dozen Cockburn's 1834 to the firm. The wine was put into Cockburn's cellars at 60 Mark Lane. Then came the war and that, for the moment, was that. We foregathered again at the beginning of 1946 at 33 Eastcheap, Mark Lane having been burnt twice in fire raids; first in the Christmas raid of 1940 and then irreparably, in May 1941. The cellar was more or less undamaged, but in the last raid was so hot that the cat got blistered feet, which shows what conditions were like from the point of view of the wine.

We therefore decided to taste through our stocks of Port starting with the oldest, the 1834, on the appropriate occasions for lunch. The wine was amber-coloured and thin; the bottles at that age varied considerably, but most were drinkable. The wines had stood up remarkably well, and really very little damage had been done. The only drawback was that after finishing the decanter, we tended to be very short tempered and to have terrible rows. After this had happened a few times, we came to the conclusion that the alcohol in the wine had taken charge and that it was rather out of balance – as indeed we were at the time.

The age at which Vintage Port is drunk is to some extent one of fashion, and also when you feel the moment for that particular year has arrived. The old rough and ready rule of twenty-one years (now I suppose eighteen), the wine having been laid down for a coming-of-age party, is as good as any other, and taking every factor into account the wine is probably at its peak of perfection. But from an everyday point of view it does seem that a particular Vintage starts being drunk and receiving general acceptance at from ten to twelve years old. The British Port drinker likes his wine to have colour and body, which a Vintage of that age will have, together with reasonable maturity. As we have seen, it will continue to give pleasure for a life span. Moreover, economics come into the picture; the longer the consumer waits, the more in real terms he will have paid for his wine.

There is some evidence from old wine lists and documents, that our grandfathers, if not our fathers, drank their Vintage at about ten years old. I started in the trade just as the great depression of the Thirties was getting under way. The fine wine-drinking class of those days was far more narrowly based than now, and these people were hard hit. Little good wine was being drunk, and stocks were, therefore, getting steadily older; hence my feeling that the age of a wine drunk may be conditioned by circumstances, which have nothing really to do with the wine itself.

I remember discussing this question on more than one occasion with my former Chairman, Fred Cockburn; the more I tried to make my point, the more he felt I should consult an alienist. However, one day after a memorable lunch, the subject came up again, and to my unconcealed delight Fred said, 'I do remember when I first came to London in 1919, I used to lunch with my old father (who had been senior partner in the firm) at the Union Club, and the tap Vintage was Cockburn's '12'. The wine was then only seven years old, and the 1912 was, and for that matter still is, no lightweight.

At about the time the 1960s were declared, some shippers began to consider whether they should not change the traditional policy of shipping in bulk to their customers and offer their Vintage in bottle only. The reasons for this reappraisal were, firstly, that the war had led to many cellars being closed, never to re-open. As old cellarmen retired, young men were reluctant to enter a trade where a long apprenticeship was required.

Secondly, because of these circumstances many firms preferred to buy in bottle, including Oporto bottlings which were greatly increasing. Thirdly, and most important, for anything as prestigious as Vintage Port, the uncertainties in the handling of postwar bottlings made some shippers prefer to take this basic and vital responsibility on their own shoulders.

Cockburn's offered their 1963 in bottle only, and though there was no great rush to follow suit, by the time the 1970 vintage came on the market probably half the total quantity was sold in bottle, and to a great extent bottled in Oporto. This was a portent of things to come, now that all future vintages must be Oporto bottled under the *Selo de Guarantia*.

What difference will bottling in Portugal make to the wine? In my view, in modern conditions, very little. Most, if not all, firms now have excellent cellars or other modern storage in Vila Nova de Gaia, and in any case, if required, the wine can be shipped over to this country, immediately after bottling, to mature. Moreover, whether we like it or not, more importance, world-wide, is being attached to bottlings in the country of origin.

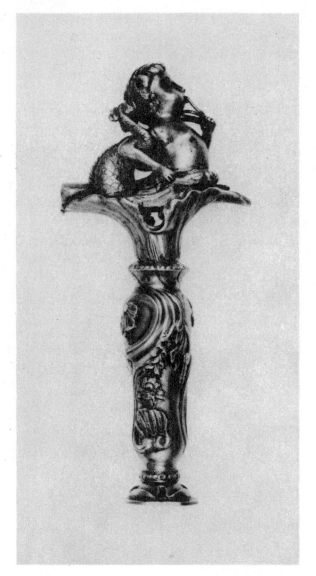

Dutch silver corkscrew *circa* 1740. The handle is formed as a triton blowing a trumpet, his tail forming a whistle. The sheath is cast and chased with rocaille and foliate motifs terminating in an octagonal seal bearing armorials. 11.3cm ($4\frac{1}{2}$ in) overall.

Some Vintage Years

Many of the following notes are extracts from contemporary notes of the period and do not relate to recent tasting.

1820 Generally regarded as a great classic.

1834 A very fine year which I have been fortunate enough to taste, as mentioned in the chapter on Vintage Port.

1847 'A very remarkable vintage, the wines so rich and well-balanced that they are still beautiful today, provided they have been well bottled and kept in a good cellar'. André L. Simon in *Port* (1934).

1851 Another great year.

1853 An exceptionally good year which never received the full appreciation its quality deserved. There was a glut of fine Vintage on the market.

1863 A magnificent vintage, rich and well-balanced. If only we could compare it with its great successor of a century later.

1868 A very fine, classic year. There was considerable debate in the trade on the rival merits of this vintage compared with the 1870s.

1870 Fine with good body; considered rather firmer than the 1868s. Declared by most shippers and was the largest vintage since 1853. I had one bottle of Cockburn 1870 which I shared in October 1976 with my young colleague from Oporto, David Orr. The wine was quite remarkable, still with some colour and fruit, the spirit not too pre-dominant. Most outstanding was the fact that after opening it continued to improve until the bottle was finished an hour later.

1872
1873 There was very considerable discussion in the trade which was the better of these two fine years, as was the case with the 1934 and 1935, which were within my memory, with

buyers' opinions probably coming down in favour of the later year.

1874 Although shipped by a small number of firms, not generally considered a good year.

1875 Fine quality, elegant but light and dry. Because of the phylloxera, which had gained a hold in the Douro region, the yield was not large.

1878 Usually considered to be the last of the pre-phylloxera years, but as the cure by grafting on American stock had not yet been discovered, the ravages of the disease were very widespread. But in spite of the poor condition of many *quintas* and a small yield, the weather for the vintage was perfect and a very great wine was produced, which rightly enjoyed a classic reputation. The Cockburn, tasted in September 1976, had the colour of Amontillado, was slightly oxidised, but still had balance and a lot of fruit developing.

1880 The wines showed considerable greenness and although offered by some firms were not generally considered very good.

1881 Generally shipped but due to the continuing difficulties with the phylloxera which had destroyed so many vines in the Cima Corgo, not a classic year.

1884 Although an attempt had now been made to cope with the phylloxera by the use of manure both natural and artificial, this was a failure and the quantity was very short; limited parcels of Vintage were however offered. Moncrieff Cockburn described his '84 as 'boot leather' because of its hardness, but having tasted the odd bottle in its extreme old age, the 'leather' had greatly mellowed and was extremely drinkable.

1885 The phylloxera difficulties continued through both years,
1886 but small quantities were offered by a minimum number of shippers.

1887 Marks the start of recovery from the phylloxera. Generally shipped and a very good year, though perhaps not quite so good as its reputation through the happy coincidence of the year being that of Queen Victoria's Golden Jubilee.

1888   Shipped by Offley, but generally considered a poor year with heavy rain before and during the vintage.

1890   A very hot year and rather dry. The wine was generally offered as a Vintage.

1892   The weather was rather similar for both these years. Too
1894   hot at the start of the vintage giving fast and furious fermentation, but rain coming just in time after the start of gathering. Both years fairly generally shipped.

1896   A very great classic year, shipped by all houses. The wine was exceptionally big and has lasted remarkably well. To me, when I first tasted the Cockburn nearly fifty years ago it was almost too big, dark and heavy. Most of the wines were drunk too early, during the First World War.

1897   Another exceptional year which would have been much more widely offered had the trade not bought such large quantities of the '96. There were those who whispered that, in view of the demand for the '96, some of the almost equally good '97 had found its way into the '96 'lots'. The vintage synchronised with Queen Victoria's Diamond Jubilee. Although Cockburn did not ship this Vintage, they supplied Harvey's of Bristol with several pipes. The wine was delicious. Sandeman also shipped an excellent wine.

1899   There were difficulties with heat and rain at the wrong times. Dow was the only firm to ship the Vintage, which they offered instead of the 1900.

1900   Of very great breed and delicacy but perhaps rather light in colour, and fine-drawn. Moncrieff Cockburn described it as 'the greatest gentleman Cockburn's ever shipped' (needless to say up to that date). I remember in my young days tasting it quite frequently and recall its beautiful fragrant and concentrated 'nose'.

1901   Shipped by Graham instead of the 1900. Not in general greatly esteemed.

1902   A good, sound year offered by Offley.

1904 This was an extraordinary vintage as most farmers produced twenty-five to thirty per cent more wine than they had allowed for. Not for the first nor indeed the last time, there was administrative bungling over the supply of brandy, and spirit had to be imported from various sources. It was said that one shipper made his Port with grain spirit from Scotland. In spite of these difficulties, good wines were made and generally the year was offered as a Vintage, though the '04 never achieved the cachet of a major classic. Cockburn's had five partners at that time, two of whom were for shipping and two against, whereupon the senior partner spun a coin to decide. It came down heads and the wine was shipped. In spite of this slightly dubious conception, the last bottle I drank was soldiering on extremely well. I remember, also, a few years back sharing an exceptional bottle of '04 Croft.

1906 A fair year shipped only by Taylor and Tuke Holdsworth.

1908 A great classic. Not a very big wine but superbly balanced with great vinosity, flavour and staying power. May still be consumed with great pleasure.

1910 Shipped by Offley only. As a year the rather uninspiring phrase 'good sound wine' fits it exactly. As 1910 is my birth year, I would have liked it to have been marked by something more notable! I have tasted the Offley at the hospitable table of their former agents, Brown Gore & Welch, and very good it was with the soft silky scent of their Boa Vista *quinta*.

1911 Sandeman shipped a famous Vintage. Also declared by Martinez and Rebello Valente.

1912 Bracketed with the '08 as one of the 'first eleven' and as such universally shipped. Certainly bigger and fruitier than the '08 and the one preferred by Ernest Cockburn – but then he liked full wines, 'black-strap', and usually referred to old Tawny as 'mouth-wash'. During all my time in the trade it has been fascinating to compare these two great wines, preferring first one, then the other. But the last time, not so many years ago, and maybe it really was the last time, I tasted them side by side. I came down on the side of the 'o8. It just seemed to have the edge in quality and 'grip' now that the fruit is fading in both wines.

1917 Good if dry and the grapes rather burnt. Shipped by several firms.

1919 A fair year with some houses offering the Vintage.

1920 Attractive wines were made and most firms shipped.

1921 Offley again the only one to declare a Vintage. Exceptionally hot weather marked the gathering.

1922 Originally rather an underrated year but as the wines grew older they developed a delightfully attractive, silky smoothness. I have enjoyed several bottles of Martinez, and just after the last war a bottle or two of Rebello Valente and Tuke.

1923 Shipped by A. J. da Silva (Noval) and Offley. Rather uneven in quality as a year but some good wines were made.

1924 A small yield but an excellent vintage. From my own experience, I would say that Taylor '24 stood out as a very great wine.

1925 A useful average year. Declared only by Offley.

1926 Offered by Kopke. Probably rather better wines than the '25s.

1927 Has proved to be one of the greatest. The wines were light when first made and some thought they lacked staying power. With development their superb quality has taken them to the top. I must admit that I have never seen a better '27 than the Cockburn. I had the privilege in November 1976 while staying with Geoffrey Beresford Smith, the retired Managing Director of Martinez, of sharing a bottle of their '27. In fruitiness, bouquet and silky finish it had everything. A very memorable experience.

1929 Offley again a 'loner' in this year. An excellent vintage, though in the heat the yield was small.

1931 A fine year which would have undoubtedly been generally shipped had it not coincided with the depths of the world slump. As it was, Noval '31, made both from the grafted vines and the very rare 'Nacional', is numbered amongst the historic Vintage Ports. It certainly brought Noval into the 'modern' first eleven.

1934
1935 Both very fine years though perhaps not quite tip-top classics and almost equally split between the firms declaring. As Cockburn shipped '35 I originally supported that year, though I never really came to terms with it until recently with the wine and the drinker in the autumn of their years. Taylor '35, though, is very good. Later I saw quite a few '34s, especially Martinez, which is a beautiful wine, silky, smooth and flavoury. I have happy memories of a delightful bottle or two of Fonseca. Perhaps for this Vintage, Sandeman had the right solution in shipping both years.

1937 Well-balanced wines with good colour and body. Burmester offered.

1938 Declared only by Taylor. Resembled the '37s but perhaps not quite so fresh and full.

1940
1941
1942
1943 A limited quantity of these years because of the war. Oporto-bottled, they were shipped over as circumstances permitted. 1942 was the Vintage offered by the greater number of firms and was probably the best. None were great years, but coming round quickly filled a gap in 'ready-to-drink' Vintage Port. They are now practically unobtainable.

1945 A very great classic year, again Oporto bottled and almost universally shipped. In 1974 I drank a Taylor '45 which has remained in my memory as one of the finest bottles of Port I have ever tasted.

1947 Shipped under the government concession, the quantity offered was small. Possibly because the wines were light in colour and body they have never quite achieved their due recognition. The fine delicate quality reminiscent of the 1900s has tended to be overlooked.

In 1975 in San Francisco, after a superb meal served with Californian wines in a private house, the guests, including myself, were asked to taste blind what turned out to be no less than four 1947 Vintage Ports, Warre, Dow, Vargellas (Taylor shipped under their *quinta* name to the U.S.A. the wine was not shipped to the U.K.) and Cockburn. I managed to keep very quiet during dinner while the Californian wines were under discussion, but was then forced into the open. Mercifully I did not entirely disgrace myself.

1948   Those who did not declare the 1947s offered the 1948s, Taylor, Graham and Fonseca in particular. Again on a personal note, I happened to be in Portugal with my firm for that vintage. It was an exceptionally hot year and we had some difficulty in keeping down the rate of the fermentations. We were therefore rather surprised when the '48s were declared. On reflection it was realised that the three firms concerned tended to have their *quintas* on the shadier south bank of the river, whereas Cockburn made most of their wine on the north side where it was certainly much hotter. Anyway, the '48, big, full and fruity, has proved a most excellent wine and extremely popular.

1950   Shipped by most of those who did not declare 1948. The wines were rather light. It could be summarised as a useful rather than a great year.

1951   Not generally regarded as vintage years, they were offered
1952   the first by Feuerheerd and the second by Kopke and Mackenzie.

1954   There is little doubt that had it not been followed by the 1955, more houses would have declared this year which had good quality, but was light in colour and body compared to the '55.

1955   Generally shipped and are magnificent wines of the very first class; big, fruity and vigorous. My personal favourite in 'modern' Vintages.

1957   Some good wines but offered only by Butler, Nephew and Mackenzie.

1958   The number of shippers and the quantity offered was small, but they were good average wines, rather light but attractive to drink. I have enjoyed some excellent bottles of Martinez.

1960   Shipped by most firms and have proved very popular. Rather similar to the 1950s but better.

1962   An excellent vintage. Offley shipped.

1963   Generally acclaimed as a great year. I must confess to being in a minority of one against the universal chorus of praise, as in the wine's younger days I was never particularly struck with it. However, as the Vintage reached maturity, my opinion changed markedly, and I have recently drunk some quite beautiful bottles of Cockburn's.

1966   With the exception of Cockburn and Martinez, very generally declared. Big wines but perhaps a little coarse.

1967   It is very difficult, in fact impossible for me to be impartial about this year, as Cockburn so very definitely preferred it to the '66. The wines are firm, with 'grip' and very great breed and style; it is not undue flattery to say they are reminiscent of the 1927s. They should be beautiful drinking when ready, and for many years to come. When our friends Taylor and Croft, after shipping the '66s, brought out their single *quinta* '67s, Vargellas and Roeda, we were very happy to say "We told you so". Martinez also preferred to offer the 1967.

1970   The weather was perfect for the vintage and a very great wine resulted, to be enjoyed to the full in the mid '80s. A considerable quantity of this Vintage was bottled in Oporto.

1972   A useful wine declared by Dow and Offley, Oporto bottled.

1975   On the light side but of good quality and should develop well for drinking in about ten years. Generally declared.

Wood Port and its World Market

To the Port shipper, his Vintage wine is a very welcome, but small and fairly infrequent 'slice of plum cake'. His business and prosperity depend basically on regular shipments of Wood Port to various markets.

By definition, Wood Port is a blended wine matured in cask until it is ready for drinking, and because it is a blend, can be, and is 'followed' by the shipper from year to year. 'So-and-so's Ruby', drunk today was the same yesterday, and will be the same tomorrow.

After the vintage gathering is completed, the new wine is left up in the Douro till the early spring of the following year, when it is racked and sent down to the shippers' lodges, *armazems*, by road or rail. The lodges are huge airy sheds with their rows of casks and vats, and roofs blackened by the fumes of evaporation. Here the wines are tasted and categorised and a start is made with the blending, which lies behind the continuity of the shippers' various 'marks'. The distinctive style of each shipper will have been basically formed by the way the wines are made and handled at the vintage, and the blending will continue this process.

There are three main types of Wood Port; Ruby, Tawny and White, with subdivisions. Ruby is easily the most popular style in this country, where the Port drinker usually likes his wine dark and full. Ruby fulfils both these conditions and is usually fairly young, so not over-expensive. A development of Ruby is called 'Vintage Character' or 'Vintage Style'. This is a wine with the same basic characteristics, but of higher quality and usually older. It will also be rather more expensive. On the question of price, it is very well worth remembering, particularly with the present exorbitant duty in Britain, that the more you are prepared to pay, the more in value of wine, as opposed to a tip for the Chancellor, you are getting out of the bottle.

'Tawny' is a well-known name in describing Port, but there often seems to be some doubt as to what it actually is. True Tawny is a description of the colour of the wine after long ageing in wood.

Port, like all red wine, loses colour in cask and in bottle too, though more slowly. Old Tawny therefore is a product of age and so can never be very low in price. A very old wine will be more expensive than many Vintages, but as a lifelong lover of old Tawny Port, I think it is a thousand pities that it is not better known and appreciated by discerning drinkers. To hold up a glass of old Tawny against a candle at the dinner table is a rare aesthetic pleasure in itself for its beautiful translucency.

Under the name 'Old Tawny' there is another wine not very often found in this country but which is popular in Europe, called 'Port with an indication of age'. The definition laid down by the Instituto do Vinho do Porto is 'A wine of 10, 15, 20, 30 or over 40 years old', and so described on the label with the date of bottling.

You note that I refer to 'true' Tawny. For many years there has been a demand for cheap Tawny Port, and by definition this must be a contradiction in terms. Shippers used to be very coy on the subject, but there is absolutely nothing to be ashamed of in saying that this style of Port is made by blending White Port with Ruby. The result is a perfectly sound, drinkable wine, but naturally it will not have the distinction conferred by age, and the colour will be more a light red or pink rather than tawny.

It is a pity that White Port which, before the last war used to have a certain vogue in this country, has gone out of fashion. Many people have never even heard of it and do not know how it is made. The answer to the latter is simple; in exactly the same way as red Port, but using white grapes. White Port like all white wine, gains colour in cask and bottle.

Most shippers have endeavoured to popularise dry White Port as an aperitif, in at least one case the wine being fermented right out, as Port was originally made, with the grape brandy added afterwards. Unfortunately, except in Portugal itself, this style of wine has had little success, although a lot of pleasure may be had, both for host and guests, in offering it well-chilled and inviting guesses as to what it is.

Ernest Cockburn is often quoted for his remark "the first duty of Port is to be red", but this was not, I believe, an anti-white blast, rather the insistence that red Port should be red and not the unattractive dull brownish tinge sometimes found in badly-made wine.

The casks and vats used for maturing are usually made of

oakwood, nowadays chiefly imported from Yugoslavia. Stainless steel, glass-lined and concrete tanks, the latter totally lined with one of the resin-based inert materials, are extensively used for blending and for storage at times when maturing is not required. Well-seasoned chestnut casks are sometimes used in the lodges, where they are quite satisfactory, but unless very carefully handled the wood is too soft to be extensively used for export. A pipe is the standard cask of the trade, holding 517 litres (115 gallons) or 56 dozen bottles, a hogshead is half a pipe and a quarter cask, half a hogshead.

The British public have been conditioned by pasteurised beer to expect wine to be bright to the last drop; the only exception being those wines which are known to require decanting, like Vintage Port. Wood Port being bottled when ready to drink, most of the deposit is thrown down in cask during maturing. Even so, after some time in bottle, it will still throw slightly, enough to make the wine cloudy when poured. To get over this problem, a considerable amount of money has been invested in various systems to prolong the bright life in bottle. The most common technique in use is to chill the wine immediately before bottling by giving it a sharp shock, causing it to throw down in a few days the deposit it would gradually lose in bottle over a period of time.

Once opened, a bottle of Wood Port will come to no harm for a considerable time provided it is firmly re-stoppered. It will certainly last as well as one of the fuller sherries. The bigger the air space in the bottle the quicker the oxidisation, so when it is half empty it is much better to finish it off! In my business life, it was not unusual after Christmas to be sent a bottle with an inch of very cloudy Port at the bottom, which the purchaser said he had opened the previous Christmas; why was it no longer fit to drink and could he please have a replacement? A suitable letter explaining the above facts had to be sent.

It was Percy Croft, of the great house of that name, who paraphrased Jorrocks in saying that any time not spent drinking Port was time wasted. He certainly put his belief into practice to the extent of about six bottles a day, starting with, as it were, a substitute for early morning tea. Wine was cheaper in those days, with a duty of only eight shillings a gallon. Croft lived to a ripe and happy old age of over eighty.

It is a pity that the English tradition is to confine Port drinking to after meals; in nearly every other country it is drunk as an aperitif and, indeed, throughout the day. While accepting the British way in general, it is worth remembering that some City bars do a roaring trade with a glass of Port mid-morning. An old Tawny, too, is delicious chilled on a hot day as an aperitif, but do not chill a full wine.

World Markets

As Port shipments to the rest of the world outside Britain are mostly of Wood Port, it may be of interest to summarise the position in some of the leading markets. There are very few countries in the world that do not import some Port, however small the quantity.

AUSTRALIA   Locally-produced Port wine types provide competition on price, but the discerning drinker on this continent still maintains a demand for the genuine product, which also applies to sherry.

BELGIUM   Ranks third in the world after France and the U.K. Consumption is biased towards Wallonia in the south, reflecting the French custom of drinking Port as an aperitif. In this sales are increased by the fact that many bars are not licensed to sell spirits, which works to the advantage of fortified wines. Despite the fact that in the North the taste for sherry develops in line with Dutch drinking habits, twice as much Port as sherry is consumed.

CANADA   A regular market, buying through individual State Liquor Control Boards, and largely following the American pattern with very strong competition from Canadian 'Port-type' wine.

DENMARK   A country, the wine trade of which is run on similar lines to that of Britain. Very good quality and with brands getting a firm hold. A little Vintage is imported.

FRANCE   This has been the largest Port market in the world since World War II, when it overtook the U.K. The most important difference compared with the U.K. is that Port is consumed as an aperitif rather than as an after-dinner drink. However, it is very much a home drink and Port occupies nearly the same position in France as sherry does in the U.K. Sherry itself is practically unknown.

GERMANY   Under seven per cent of adults drink Port regularly, so the potential is considerable.

HOLLAND   A good market though price conscious. U.K. brands are gaining an increasing acceptance. As in most countries Port is chiefly drunk as an aperitif. I remember travelling in Holland in 1950 with our agent, and calling on one of our customers, with whom we were to have lunch. "Ah" said our host, "I have an aperitif which you as an Englishman will particularly enjoy". That aperitif turned out to be a bottle of Cockburn 1947, one year in bottle. We finished a bottle between the three of us and sat down to a monumental Dutch lunch none the worse.

ITALY   Formerly hardly any Port was used, but of recent years a good trade has grown up, entirely imported in bottle.

NEWFOUNDLAND   A very small market, but of historical interest as casks of Port, shipped by Hunt Roope, first found their way there as ballast in the holds of the Newman family's cod-fishing fleet. The wine was so improved by the trip, that a storage bond was set up in Newfoundland.

NORWAY/SWEDEN/FINLAND/ICELAND   All these Scandinavian countries control liquor buying and sales through government monopolies. All were strong buyers of Port, but, alas, times have changed. Some liberalisation of licensing laws have led to spirits being more competitive, while *ad valorem* duties on the increased cost of Port have tended to price it out of the market. It is of interest to note that both Iceland and Norway used large quantities of White Port; in Norway drunk as a 'chaser' after beer.

PORTUGAL   The Portuguese themselves are not great Port drinkers, but have begun to drink more of recent years. The advent of tourism has now made Portugal one of the best markets on a *per capita* basis. Dry White Port is popular.

RUSSIA   In Tsarist times very high quality White Port was supplied for the Court and aristocracy. Until recently Cockburn shipped a small quantity of this same mark to Sweden. The Cockburn partner who travelled Russia was always given a fur coat by the firm – almost the only 'perk' they gave in those days.

Curiously, there is now a revival of trade with the U.S.S.R.

SOUTH AFRICA   As in North America and Australia, there is strong competition from locally-produced Port-style wines. Nevertheless, there is a small trade for imported Port, with a surprising preference shown for the White.

SOUTH AMERICA   All countries buy Port from time to time, imports largely depending on the somewhat fluctuating state of their economies. Brazil, with her Portuguese ancestry, is the most important.

SWITZERLAND   Port sells in French Switzerland, largely by the litre to restaurants and cafés.

THE UNITED STATES   In the old New England States Port had to compete with Madeira. American Port (there is no protection of the word as in the United Kingdom) has a considerable sale, at about a quarter the price of the imported wine, but it has a poor social image, which reflects very much on the Portuguese product. To combat this all Port bottled in Portugal is now labelled 'Porto', though historically a large proportion of imported Port is bottled in and re-exported from England. This wine is still, as before, labelled 'Port'.

The Factory House and British Clubs

The somewhat archaic-sounding title of Factory House, applied to what is now in fact a private club, stems from the eighteenth century when British trade was expanding in many parts of the world. In several ports, through which passed both the exports of the country concerned and imports from England, British merchants or 'Factors' set up their own trade organisation and held their meetings in the house of either the British Consul or in that of one of their own members. These 'Factories' existed in Portugal at Viana, Lisbon and Oporto.

In Oporto the Factory, after 1814, became known as the British Association, and under the chairmanship of the Consul administered two 'contribution funds'. One for exports to the United Kingdom in British ships had financed the building of the Factory House, while the 'inward' fund, levied on all imports from the same source, was used to pay the Consul, the British Chaplain and to give any necessary assistance to distressed British subjects and similar deserving causes for charity. This system furthermore entailed the employment of a British Customs Officer, and was, therefore, very naturally disliked by the host nation. The British Association of Oporto, with its Factory House, has become the last of its kind in Europe, though it has long ceased to perform its original function.

The treaty of 1654 between Dom João IV of Portugal and Cromwell's Commonwealth was the foundation for the English commercial supremacy in Portugal. England was allowed to trade with the Portuguese colonies, importing slaves from Africa and coffee from Brazil, but above all the English merchants of the Factories in Lisbon and Oporto were granted what would now be called 'extra-territorial' rights. The merchants were exempt from new taxes, from arrest unless caught red-handed in criminal activity, and Portuguese courts had no jurisdiction over their property.

Perhaps most important of all, in a strongly Catholic country, they were given permission to hold Protestant services in their houses and on board ship, and in 1784 they were allowed their own cemetery, Consul Whitehead being deputed to look for a suitable site. The establishment of a strong British community in Oporto dates from the Cromwellian treaty. The favourable political and commercial climate led to the merchants of the Factory setting up their homes in Portugal instead of coming out for business on a single voyage and returning to England.

Thus was laid the foundation of what was to become the Port Wine trade. At this stage the Factory merchants, in what was called, curiously to modern ears, the 'rag trade', were engaged largely in selling cotton, wool and general merchandise to the Portuguese in exchange for oil and fruit. The protectionist policy of Louis XIV's minister, Colbert, inaugurated in 1667, gave the opportunity to the now resident English to open up a wine trade based initially on the thin wines of Monsão in the north of Portugal, and exported through Viana do Castelo.

The Factors were tough and independent men, and being strong Royalists gave Cromwell's Consul Maynard a difficult time. With the Restoration this source of friction disappeared, but the early part of the eighteenth century saw the disorders of the War of the Spanish succession, with an English force under Lord Galway stationed in the north of the country. Inevitably the troops were frequently drunk, and their behaviour made the journey between Oporto and Viana even more hazardous than did the more normal perils of the native highwaymen and brigands.

In spite of these comparatively minor annoyances life was good, and the English, as they have always been wont to do, kept to the way of life which they would have followed at home, indulging in the same amusements. Sundays, as well as Divine Service, saw cock-fighting, cards and wine-drinking in the evening. Moreover their creature comforts tended to be looked after by well-trained English-speaking black servants; ships trading with the American colonies frequently called in at Oporto on the way home, and a slave would be bartered for a pipe of wine.

In 1727 the British Factors in Oporto for the first time drew up a set of rules and regulations for their various trades, both for import and export. In the wine trade these were directed to improvements in the trade and to keep down the prices paid to the growers. The English taste, as it is and always has been, was for full, dark wine, and in a good year the big pre-phylloxera wines of the Douro gave all that was required. But as trade increased the inevitable occurred, vines were planted in less good situations, with a consequent lowering of quality. The remedy, unfortunately, was to adulterate the wine in some form or another. Lower quality wines were boosted with sugar, rather haphazardly dosed with brandy, and *baga* (elderberry juice) was widely used to give extra colour. The shippers themselves were adding brandy, before shipment, to give the wine stamina for the voyage to England.

The Merchants of the Factory objected to the growers' practice of adding brandy during fermentation (present-day Port had not yet been invented). The growers replied with a devastating retort, saying in so many words that any adulteration was at the instigation of the Factory. The flood of bad wine continued and, as always happens in like situations, the boom broke and the prices slumped. In 1755 a pipe of Douro wine was down to between £2 and £3, and the Factors were saying that unless adulteration was stopped they would not even taste the wines let alone buy them.

The growers, thoroughly frightened by this threat, came down to the Factory in a body and offered their wines at any price the buyer would pay. The shippers still refused to buy, and the growers in desperation went down to Lisbon and placed a copy of the Factory letter on adulteration in the hands of the great Portuguese Prime Minister, the Marquis de Pombal.

The Factory had overplayed its hand. For some time the Marquis, jealous of the English commercial hegemony and the virtual monopoly of the lucrative wine trade, had been casting round for a suitable curb to their pretensions. The recklessly arrogant Factory letter gave him the pretext he wanted, and its publication in Lisbon led to a furious outbreak of anglophobia; it was even alleged that the shippers required *droit de seigneur* of the farmers' daughters as part payment for their wine. The Marquis de Pombal decreed the remedy. A state monopoly company was to be set up, through which all wine was to be bought at fixed prices. Horror-struck, a deputation from the Factory hurried to Lisbon to protest but in vain. The Minister was adamant, and in 1756 the Companhia Geral da Agricultura dos Vinhos do Alto Douro, the 'Old Company', was set up with full control, and the wine-growing area of the Douro divided into two categories, the best for export, known as 'Factory' wine, and the second grade for consumption in Portugal. Nationalisation has a long ancestry.

By the end of the century, prosperity, in which the Douro farmers joined, had returned to the trade, and the power of the 'Old Company' had waned. The English Factors were again living off the fat of the land, eating the same quantity of food and drinking the same amount of wine as their contemporaries in Britain. The British community had greatly expanded and many of today's firms were now in existence, Warre, Croft, Taylor, Offley and Sandeman among them. Of the non-British Houses, Kopkes, van Zeller and Burmester also flourished.

Between 1786 and 1790, John Whitehead, Consul to the Factory, supervised the building of that monument to English self-confidence in the future of the trade, the Factory House, headquarters of the British Association in Oporto. Unostentatious and in solid Georgian style that would not have been out of place in Regency Bath, it epitomised the 'Rule Britannia' sentiments of those days.

It is perhaps significant that the Treasurer of the Factory during the building of the House was John Croft, of the old established wine firm. The Factory House was to be used as an office for the Consul, for officials of the Association, for meetings to discuss the administration of the contribution fund, for entertaining distinguished local figures, and it was certainly also used as a club. Paid for by the fund to which many of the newly-arrived British merchants had subscribed – indeed they had no option to do otherwise – they were not, with typical snobbery, to be allowed by the older members of the Association to enjoy the amenities of the new building.

In March 1809 Oporto was captured by Marshal Soult's French army but the French enjoyment of 'liberated' Port did not last long. In May the city was relieved by Wellington (Sir Arthur Wellesley as he then was), who with his staff was able to enjoy Soult's dinner thoughtfully prepared at the Palace of the Carrancas. The French started their long retreat through Portugal, ending in Soult's defeat at Talavera.

The Factory House had been requisitioned by the French, and on their departure a Senhor Queiroz re-opened it as a coffee shop. However, on 11 November 1811, on the eviction of Queiroz, eleven shippers, eating eleven courses and drinking eleven wines, sat down to a ceremonial opening dinner. In the succeeding years many senior army officers were dined there, all signing the Visitors'

Pressing: old . . .
. . . and new

The new wine

The concrete storage tanks and the traditional pipes

The peace of the lodge

The coopers

Book. Until the end of the war there was a constant coming and going of British officers, all this doubtless of future benefit to the Port trade.

Not surprisingly the war years had been disastrous for the trade; shipments had been suspended and the vineyards, where not fought over, had been untended. But with the permanent disappearance of the French in Spain, in 1811 things began to get back to normal. In 1815 Cockburn's name first appears on the list of shippers, followed by Graham's in 1820, a year that heralded a succession of remarkably fine Vintages. But the year also heralded an internecine quarrel which broke out amongst members of the British community over the right to use the Factory House. The cause was a typical one; the old 'aristocracy' of the British Association, now mostly Port shippers, denied membership to the 'parvenus', or most recent arrivals who in general dealt in commodities other than wine.

The quarrel reached such a pitch of bitterness that in 1825 the excluded merchants addressed a Memorial to Prime Minister Canning. In this they complained that the administration of the contribution had fallen entirely into the hands of a club, the British Association, who were in possession of the Factory House, and who had admitted as new members only those who were members of the wine trade. The Memorialists claimed that this was a business and social stigma, and that their election was at the mercy of the traditional one black ball in the ballot box. Poor Memorialists! Canning refused to accept their plea; the *status quo* and the 'closed shop' remain triumphant to this day.

Members of the Factory House and the Memorialists were soon involved in far more serious and widespread troubles, the Civil War of the Brothers. In 1820 a radical revolt, particularly supported in the north of the country including Oporto, gained Portugal for the first time a constitution and a parliament. But in 1828 the absolutist Prince Miguel took over the throne, repealing the constitution. Oporto supported his liberal brother Pedro, heartily abetted by the British community, but in 1829 the Miguelites took over the city, executing a number of leading citizens, while even some of the British, including Charles Noble of Warre, were imprisoned. In 1832 Dom Pedro, the ex-Emperor of Brazil, landed north of Oporto to win back the crown for his daughter Maria da Gloria from Dom Miguel.

At this news the Miguelites panicked and evacuated Oporto, which perhaps was fortunate, for when the citizens stood ready to cheer the entry of Dom Pedro's army they were not particularly impressed by what they saw. Not only was it far fewer in numbers than the recently departed Miguelites, but it was composed of a curiously assorted collection of an international character: regular Portuguese *caçadores*, a students' battalion and units of various nationalities, prompted by ideals of liberty as well as more mercenary considerations; English and French, many of whom had fought in the Napoleonic armies, mingled with Germans and Dutch. Strangest of all was a Scottish contingent under Colonel Shaw, recruited largely from the Gorbals, usually drunk, and equally terrible to friend and foe.

Recovering their poise, the Miguelites besieged this motley collection in Oporto, a siege that was to endure for over a year. For some reason the River Douro was never closed by the Miguelites and, though Vila Nova da Gaia was in their hands, enterprising shippers like young J. J. Forrester of Offley's were able to slip across the river from time to time to see that all was well in the lodges.

On the whole the English did not greatly suffer in their substantial houses, though Mr. Wright of Croft's had to undergo the amputation of an arm after a shell came through the ceiling of his dining-room as he was enjoying a glass of Port. As usual in these circumstances, the poor had a bad time and casualties, many of them children, were heavy. General depression was settling in amongst both defending troops and civilians when news came, in June 1833, of the complete defeat of the Miguelites off Cape St. Vincent by Dom Pedro's fleet, commanded by Admiral Charles Napier. In July the final assault on Oporto was broken. That night *Te Deums* were sung in the churches, and the British Association held a dance in the Factory House. The war was won, but as a last gesture of defiance the Miguelites blew up a lodge in Vila Nova de Gaia, causing a fire which only prompt action by British seamen kept from spreading to other lodges. As it was, 2,700 pipes of Port ran in streams down to the Douro, turning the whole river a muddy ruby.

On 4 September the members of the British Association sat down to dine in the battered Factory House for the first time in eighteen months since the siege began. The next year J. J. Forrester painted his famous picture of the shippers conversing happily together outside the Factory House in the Rua Nova dos Ingleses. But the storm brewed up by Forrester in his charges of adulteration of Port and his plea for the cessation of fortification was about to break *(see page 79)*.

The restoration of peace after the Forrester tempest saw the Golden Age of Port, with the greatest emphasis on Vintage. The Factory House shared in these glories to the full. A lot of money was being made out of the Port trade, and was reflected in the standard of living and entertainment. Sport flourished, including rowing, shooting and, of course, cricket, with a dinner at the Factory always following the annual match, W. R. Teage's XI v. H. Murat's XI.

The boom in Port after the First World War was in its extremes somewhat unhealthy and, followed by the depression and consequent change in drinking habits led to much shaking of heads among the British shippers. However, by 1934, after a bad period when no dances were held at the Factory House, things were looking up and a highly successful ball was given in that year. But although business was quite good, the British market, the quality side of the trade, had declined by fifty per cent.

The trade continued and survived almost complete cessation during the Second World War. Today in terms of volume France is now much the biggest market, taking nearly twice as much Port as Britain, but the Factory House has survived unchanged and indomitable. Dances and dinners are still held with due state and formality, even though dress is dinner-jacket and soft shirt instead of the earlier white tie and tails; for the formal dinner both identical dining-rooms are used, the company moving into the second room in order to enjoy their Port uncontaminated by the smell of food.

The member firms of the Association (and very proud of the fact) are Cockburn, Croft, Delaforce, Gonzalez Byass, Graham, Guimaraens, Martinez Gassiot, Offley Forrester, Robertson, Sandeman, Silva & Cosens, Taylor and Warre.

The Treasurer, who is, in fact, the Chairman, is elected for one year at a time in turn from the resident members, and during that time the Treasurer's firm supplies the Wood Ports for all occasions. The great day of the Factory week is the regular Wednesday lunch, which usually sees a good turn-out of Association members and their guests, (which – ungallantly – does not include ladies). The

Treasurer chooses the Vintage Port for the lunch from the Factory House cellars, and there is great enjoyment in trying to guess the shipper and the year.

Built of solid granite, the Factory is certainly cool in summer, if cold in winter, and a great feature is the superb unsupported granite staircase from the vestibule to the mezzanine. The Factory's Writing Room and Visitors' Book go back to 1812: its library contains some 20,000 volumes. On the main floor are the twin dining-rooms and a magnificent ballroom with crystal chandeliers. The House contains much fine, traditional furniture, though it is unlikely, as has sometimes been stated, that the drawing-room chairs were made by Chippendale or a contemporary. Chippendale himself died in 1779, before the building of the Factory House. Some beautiful china is on display, the oldest set being a Spode tea service. The origin of the dessert service has been attributed to Coalport, but experts have not been able to confirm this. The whole atmosphere of the Factory House is one of tradition and old-fashioned solidarity.

The Factory House had the great honour of the first visit by a reigning British Sovereign, when the British Association had the privilege of receiving Queen Elizabeth II, accompanied by the Duke of Edinburgh, in February 1957. They were shown round by the Treasurer of that year, Charles Guimaraens of Graham's.

The Oporto British Club & the Oporto Cricket & Lawn Tennis Club

The Oporto British Club was founded in 1904, comparatively late in the history of the community. It certainly owes its inception in part to jealousy caused by the Factory House 'closed shop', although many members of the Factory House were also founder members of the O.B.C. A fine house was purchased in the Virtudes (Street of the Virtues, not entirely felicitously named, as it was to a considerable extent inhabited by ladies of the town), surrounded by a part of the old city wall. The house was surmounted by a flagpole from which the Union Jack was flown on ceremonial occasions.

From the first, with 135 full members, the club prospered though there were the conventional difficulties over certain people being black-balled, but these matters were eventually smoothed over. Bridge and billiards flourished, as did more social activities such as wedding receptions. In 1908 the committee had the honour of entertaining the young King of Portugal, Manoel II.

As an example of conservative thinking, a proposal that a bar should be installed was defeated at an Extraordinary General Meeting in 1925 by twenty-nine votes to nine; although in all fairness it must be stated that the consumption of Port at the club was not adversely affected.

In 1967 it was decided for a variety of reasons to amalgamate the O.B.C. with the Oporto Cricket and Lawn Tennis Club, in newly-rebuilt premises. Though one must tread warily in such matters, I personally think it was the right decision.

The Cricket Club was founded in 1855, and moved to its present quarters at the Campo Alegre (The Field) in about 1860, and there cricket is still played on a grass wicket, the only one in Portugal. In Lisbon they play on matting.

When Alan Tait, the then Honorary Secretary, wrote to *The Times* in March 1955 to note the club's centenary, he also took the opportunity of asking for details of any clubs outside Great Britain with a longer history. This started a lively correspondence from which it transpired that, though there are older clubs in India, Hong Kong and Alexandria, besides several in the U.S.A. and Canada, Oporto holds the palm for longevity on the continent of Europe.

The great event of the season is the Test Match between Oporto and Lisbon, played alternately on the two clubs' grounds. There are frequent visits from sides from England, the first match having been against the Channel Squadron in 1863. Since then the Cryptics, Gentlemen of Worcester, Dorset Rangers and private sides, some very strong, have been made welcome. Last, but not least, there have been several visits from Wine Trade XI's, in three of which I was lucky enough to play. On paper the visitors sometimes looked to be overwhelmingly powerful, but lunch and out-of-hours entertainment from their hospitable hosts usually levelled things up pretty well, so that Oporto were not disgraced.

Tennis has also flourished, and the rebuilding of the Club House with a squash court in the basement has been matched by new tennis courts, and a swimming pool which is the particular delight of members' children. The Club House is extremely comfortable and well-run, and the dining-room first-class.

Between the wars, both codes of football were played on The Field, soccer on Saturdays and rugby on Sundays. When I did my year in Oporto in 1932–33 we could still hold our own against some Portuguese soccer teams by adopting what we rather speciously described as Corinthian tactics, but times have changed. The British community also taught the Portuguese to play rugby, but the shortage of men during the war put a stop to the game and it was never revived.

The most dangerous game of the year should not go unrecorded, the mixed hockey matches of Gentlemen v. Ladies, an indeterminate number on both sides, on Christmas afternoon.

Some Port Shippers

BARROS ALMEIDA & CO.   This firm now controls one of the largest groups of companies in the Port trade. They own several firms, including the Douro Wine Shippers Association and have large table wine interests. Senhor Manuel de Barros came to the top in the classic tradition, starting his business life at the age of fourteen as an office boy, becoming office manager at eighteen and a year later marrying his boss's daughter. He died full of years and honour, and the business is now carried on by his two sons, Manuel and João.

BORGES & IRMAO.   One of the older Portuguese firms. Today the Portuguese Government are shareholders. Their table wine trade is particularly important.

J. W. BURMESTER & CO.   Founded in 1730 by two partners, John Nash, an Englishman and Burmester, a German, under the style of Burmester Nash & Co. In 1784 a younger son of the house of Ormonde, James Butler, went out to Oporto as clerk to the firm. In 1789 the partnership was dissolved by mutual consent and Burmester started his own business as Burmester & Co. One of the smaller firms, but highly respected, it is run by Senhor Armando Silva.

BUTLER, NEPHEW & CO.   The firm was started by Nash of Burmester who took the young James Butler into partnership in 1789. On Nash's death, Butler took into partnership his nephew, John Tyndale, the style becoming Butler, Tyndale & Co. In 1809 a Mr. Naylor became a partner, and the firm changed its name to Butler, Naylor & Co. James Butler then admitted as a partner his nephew, Robert Butler, and the name of the firm became as it is at present. In 1845 Samuel Dixon was made a partner, and on his death in 1897, his three sons became owners of the firm.

It is of interest that before the last war, though Butler, Nephew shipments were very small and limited to four or five large customers, their minimum price was £70 per pipe F.O.B. at a time when Port could be bought in bond in London for as little as £16 per pipe. The quality of their wines was superb.

Butler, Nephew is now owned by Gonzalez Byass & Co.

A. A. CALEM & CO.   One of the great Portuguese shippers, still wholly a family business and now directed by Dr. Joaquim Manuel Calem. The firm is particularly strong in their home market, but is well spread in many others.

COCKBURN SMITHES & CO.   Robert Cockburn, younger brother of Henry, Lord Cockburn, the famous Scottish judge who made his name as an advocate in the trial of Burke and Hare, had served in the Peninsular War, and thus had the opportunity of seeing the possibilities of Portugal as a wine-growing country.

With his great friend, George Wauchope of Leith, he founded the firm in 1815, and married Mary Duff, whom Lord Byron much admired. It is of interest that David Orr, one of the present directors, is married to Susan Duff, a member of the family.

In 1828 Captain William Greig of the Merchant Service joined the two partners, and the firm became Cockburn, Wauchope & Greig. A few years later, maintaining the sea-faring tradition, Captain (later Admiral) Hugh Dunlop, R.N., who married a Miss Cockburn, was admitted. He must have had extended leave of absence from the firm during the Crimean War, for he commanded a ship with his brother-in-law as a guest on board.

Robert Cockburn died in 1854, leaving his two sons Archibald and Alexander to carry on the business. Regrettably it must be said that Archibald found it necessary to write some very strong letters to his younger brother, drawing attention to his idleness and general lack of interest in the business.

Henry Smithes, having started his business career in the Union Bank at the age of fifteen, went to Oporto and became a partner in 1854 when Dunlop left the business. Henry, having introduced his younger brother John T. Smithes into the firm, returned to the London office, leaving his brother in Oporto. The style of the firm then became Cockburn Smithes & Co.

J. T. Smithes married twice, first Miss Margaret Teage and secondly Miss Eleanor Cobb, a sister of C. D. Cobb his London partner, thereby introducing both families into the firm. W. R. Teage took over from John Smithes, and J. L. Teage Jnr. from his uncle, who in turn, on his retirement, handed over to W. M. Cobb, who had to be sent for from Australia because of the lack of male heirs.

W. M. Cobb was followed by his son R. M. (Reggie) Cobb, who has only recently retired as Chairman. During his great service to the firm and to Anglo-Portuguese relations he has been awarded the Portuguese Ordem de Cristo, the O.B.E., and is now C.B.E. He has had as his colleagues, first A. C. Smithes, son of J. T., and then my contemporary John H. Smithes, son of A. C., together with a cousin of the Cobbs', Felix Vigne. One may say with certainty that in their respective epochs, there were no finer tasters of Port than A. C. and J. H. Smithes, father and son.

After the war, and with the return of John Smithes and Felix Vigne from the R.A.F., Trevor Heath from Delaforce joined the firm and soon the Board. Retirements now loomed, R.M. Cobb becoming non-executive Chairman, and J. H. Smithes Consultant, with Trevor Heath and Antonio Filipe, the accountant, joint Managing Directors. On Heath's retirement due to ill-health, Antonio Filipe was joined on the Board by David B. Orr, and Gordon Guimaraens from Martinez Gassiot, that firm being under the same umbrella as Cockburn's.

In London the fort was held chiefly by Cockburns, interspersed with Cobbs. Senior members of the trade will remember the towering figure of Ernest Cockburn, Senior Partner and then Chairman from 1929-1938. He was succeeded by his cousin Fred Cockburn, equally well-known, who retired in 1964. Captain Frank Ree, R.N. came in after the 1914-1918 war, and was made a director with Colin C. Gordon in 1931. Both Colin Gordon and I are cousins of Ernest Cockburn on the distaff side. (No nonsense about family connections!)

After the war it became obvious that the firm must look for friends with whom to consolidate the business. Harvey's now handle the brand brilliantly and, while greatly increasing the sales, they have preserved the essential reputation for quality on which the name of Cockburn is founded.

COMPANHIA VELHA Descended from the Marquis de Pombal's monopoly company. The wheel having turned full circle the firm is now once again under government control.

CROFT & CO. Certainly one of the oldest Port houses founded as Phayre & Bradley in 1678. The first Croft appears in 1736 when the name of the firm had been transformed to Tilden Thompson & Croft. John Croft came from York where he continued to carry on his business as wine merchant.

Another John Croft went to Portugal during the Peninsular War. There he met his old friend William Warre and later married Warre's sister, Amelia. At considerable personal risk he carried on intelligence work in north Portugal, concerned with the movements of the French armies. For these services he was created a baronet. He was responsible for organising the distribution of the British gift of £100,000 to the Portuguese who had suffered from the war.

The lure of the life of country gentleman in the North of England proved too strong for the Crofts, who all returned home during the early part of the nineteenth century, and the management of the business was taken over by the Wright family.

A story is told of J. R. Wright, the first of the clan, which well illustrates the business ethics of the day. The summer of 1868 was excessively hot, and when Mr. Wright visited the Douro he found that the grapes were ripe enough to pick but so small and parched by the sun that they could not be expected to give a Vintage of substance either in quality or quantity. Mr. Wright reported this on his return to his friends and competitors at the Factory House. What, however, he could not know was that from the day he set out on muleback to return to Oporto, a fine, warm rain had been falling steadily day and night, swelling the grapes and in fact transforming the 1868s into one of the greatest Vintages ever made. All shippers declared a '68 except Croft. Mr. Wright had given his word that the year would not be shipped, and nothing would make him break it for the first time in his life.

Shortly after the 1914–18 war the firm was incorporated into Gilbey's, which has now expanded into the International Distillers and Vintners.

Since that time Croft's have been fortunate in having a succession of well-known and able managers, Hugh Watson, George (Chico) Robertson, Basil Kendall and now Robin Reid. They own the well-known Quinta da Roeda at Pinhão, originally bought from Taylor's.

In 1952, Croft bought the old firm of Morgan Bros. I was delighted to hear that Croft was considering re-offering the old Morgan brand 'Dixon's Double Diamond', mentioned by Dickens in *Nicholas Nickleby*.

DELAFORCE SONS & CO.   John Fleurriet Delaforce was born on 8 September 1807 in Tooley Street, Southwark, London. He first came to Oporto in September 1834 to the firm of Martinez Gassiot & Co. and had probably been in their London office. He was of Huguenot origin, as were the Gassiot's, He thus started his work in Oporto at the age of twenty-seven, and continued until his death there on 4 August 1881, having been manager of Martinez Gassiot for many of those years.

Sadly, many of the records of Martinez were lost through fire in the London Blitz of the Second World War, but a letter exists dated 12 February 1842 acknowledging an invoice of 172 pipes of wine selected for them by Mr. Delaforce, from Messrs. Cockburn Greig & Co. – a forerunner of future partnership in the following century.

John Delaforce's second son, George Henry, was born in Oporto on 11 July 1844, and he started the present Delaforce business as we know it today when he began trading under his own name in 1886, at the age of twenty-four. His eldest son, Henry John, was born in the same year, which must have been eventful for his young father, being also in the middle of the phylloxera scourge and the year of Disraeli's first term as Prime Minister.

Shipments were made by George Henry to many European markets, especially to the United Kingdom, Norway, Denmark, Germany and Russia, and he also had the honour of being appointed a supplier to the Portuguese Royal House in 1894. There is a photograph of his lodges of that time at 11 Queimados (now Rua Barão de Forrester) showing wooden cases with the Royal Arms, which are still used by the firm today.

George Henry Delaforce's sons, Henry and Reginald, formed the partnership of Delaforce Sons & Co. on 1 July 1903 when their father ceased trading under his individual name. Their agents in England were Merritt Bird & Co. of Mark Lane. There was also a London Office at 110 Cannon Street, which was later transferred to 16 Water Lane, above the offices of Martin Bird, Hallowes & Co. who were appointed agents in 1921.

Reginald Delaforce died suddenly in Oporto in 1925 at the early age of fifty-one, after working for the latter part of his life in Portugal and having helped considerably to expand the business in the boom years immediately after the First World War, especially with the famous Vintages of 1917, 1919 and 1922.

Henry Delaforce lived in England, mainly London, from 1913 until his death there in 1946, and he came to Oporto regularly during this time. In 1931 he purchased from the Barbosa family the Quinta de Foz de Temilobos on the Régua to Pinhão road, and a wine-making centre was subsequently constructed there. He also made regular visits to agents and customers in the United Kingdom and Eire, and was a keen follower of racing, winning several events with his horses.

Henry's sons, Victor and John, joined the firm in 1922 and 1931 respectively, the former being responsible for all aspects of wine production and tasting, and the latter for the financial side and the international sales development of the Delaforce brand, having both probably visited more countries than anyone in the Port trade. They lived in Oporto and directed the business until the end of the 1960s, apart from a period of absence during the Second World War. Victor's son Patrick was with the firm between 1947 and 1953, as was Trevor Heath, who later joined Cockburn Smithes and is the son of Frank Heath, general manager in Oporto for Delaforce from 1918 to 1951.

In 1968, the company became part of the International Distillers and Vintners Ltd. of London, formed a few years previously by the merger of United Wine Traders and Gilbey's. Twiss, Brownings & Hallowes, a member of United Wine Traders, had been Delaforce agents from 1926–1963. The company has continued to expand as one of the principal international Port names. At the time of writing, John Delaforce's sons David (joined in 1958) and Richard (1968) are responsible as Managing and Marketing Director, and Sales Manager respectively, and thus continue the long family connections with Port and Oporto.

DOW & CO., *see* SILVA & COSENS

A. A. FERREIRA   Founded in 1761, the firm had no more than a local reputation until the famous widow Dona Antonia Ferreira took up the reins. Born at Régua in 1810, she died at an advanced age worth the equivalent of more than £3,000,000.

Twice married and twice widowed, she married first her cousin A. B. Ferreira, one of the richest men in Portugal at that time. On his death she married the very able manager of the properties, Francisco Torres. When she became a widow for the second time she took the whole administration into her own hands.

Still the owners of several beautiful properties, of which the Quinta do Vesuvio is probably the best, the firm is one of the largest and best-known of the Portuguese Port shippers.

Dona Antonia was in the Douro boat with Baron Forrester when the latter was drowned in the Cachão rapids in 1862. She was kept afloat by her expanse of crinoline, and happily saved.

FEUERHEERD BROS. & CO.   This firm was founded in 1815 by a young man only twenty-two years of age, D. M. Feuerheerd. In those days the house carried on a business as general merchants exporting in particular large numbers of cattle, also oranges and other products to Great Britain. Feuerheerd was also one of the pioneers of steam navigation between Portugal and England.

In 1849 D. M. Feuerheerd retired and was succeeded by his two sons, D. M. Feuerheerd Jnr. and H. L. Feuerheerd, the latter becoming the sole owner in 1881, when he converted the firm from general merchants to concentrate his energies entirely as a Port wine shipper. He became one of the best-known figures in the trade, and one of the original members of the Wine & Spirit Trade's Benevolent Society.

His son, Albert M. Feuerheerd, joined the firm in 1890 and became equally well-known in Port wine circles. He died suddenly in 1933. I have happy memories of more than one superb dinner at his hospitable table.

The firm was sold to Barros Almeida, but their famous Quinta la Rosa remains in the family, having been run for a great many years by Mr. Feuerheerd's daughter, the late Mrs. Claire Bergqvist, who kept up to the fullest extent the family's reputation for viticulture and hospitality.

FONSECA   *see* GUIMARAENS

GONZALEZ BYASS & CO.   Opened in Oporto in 1896 as an off-shoot of the great sherry house. They secured the invaluable services of Herbert Pheysey, son of the wine-buyer of the Army & Navy Stores, to open the office and act as manager. Cecil Pheysey succeeded his father in 1934 and retired in 1960.

In 1940, under the threat of possible invasion of the Iberian Peninsular by Hitler, Manola Gonzalez, third son of the Marquess de Torre Soto and a director of the parent company, was sent from Spain as a precautionary measure. He has continued to divide his time between Jerez and Oporto.

From 1901 until the mid '30s the firm had an arrangement with the van Zeller family to buy the production of their famous Quinta Roriz, and Gonzalez Byass vintages were shipped under that name.

GUIMARAENS VINHOS S.A.R.L.   Although it is known that Fonseca Monteiro & Co. existed well back in the eighteenth century, it was not until 1822 that Manuel Pedro Guimaraens acquired the business, which in those days was trading principally with Brazil. Shortly afterwards, the head office was moved to London, where it remained for over a hundred years, and M. P. G. Guimaraens married an Englishwoman who bore him three sons, all born and educated in England. The three sons, who all joined the business, progressively built up the English market as well as those in Scandinavia and the Low Countries. Well before the turn of the century, Fonseca (the brand derived from the original name of the firm) was enjoying a fine reputation, particularly for Vintage Ports.

From 1896 to 1949 the firm was run by Frank and George Guimaraens. Frank made every Fonseca Vintage from 1896 to 1948, a span covering fifty-two years, which must be unique in the trade. In 1949 the Yeatman family of Taylor Fladgate bought the firm. Bruce Guimaraens joined in 1956.

Another Guimaraens, Pat, entered the family business in 1926 till 1939, when he joined the R.A.F.V.R. After the war he worked in London with the firm's agent looking after the selling side.

Fonseca continues to be one of the leading names in Port, selling in more than forty countries around the world.

W. J. GRAHAM & CO.   Graham's was founded as a dry goods and, in particular, textile business in the early 1820s. The firm also had extensive interests in India. Legend has it that in 1826 the Oporto office accepted payment of a debt in Port, thereby entering the trade and becoming Port shippers.

Owners of the beautiful Quinta Malvedos, near neighbours of Cockburn's at Tua, they were particularly strong in Scotland where for many years they had their own office. The firm is very well known for its Vintage, ranking certainly in the first half-dozen.

When I first went out to Oporto in 1932, Max Graham and his brother Gerard were the senior partners, and their hospitality is memorable. Gerard was a great collector, and his downstairs cloakroom was full of objects taken from similar rooms in British railway trains. The story goes that lacking only a railway lavatory-seat for his collection he unscrewed one in a Scottish express, put it over the crook of his arm, and, proffering his ticket with the same hand, walked past the astonished ticket-collector.

Graham's were recently bought by the Symington family of Silva & Cosens. Finally it should be chronicled that at one time, of Graham's Glasgow Board of five members, two held the V.C. – Lt. Col. Sir Reginald Graham Bt., V.C., C.B.E., and Brigadier Lorne Campbell V.C., D.S.O.

HUNT ROOPE & CO. LTD.   Has perhaps the longest and most romantic history of any firm in Oporto. Its origins centre round the old Devon and Dartmouth families of Newman, Roope, Holdsworth, Hunt and Teage (their Vintage brand is Tuke Holdsworth); the Newmans did business with their own ships in dried codfish *(bacalhau)* and wine as long ago as the fifteenth century. By 1679 they were bartering Newfoundland cod for Portuguese wine which was found to have been greatly improved by maturing on the voyage. This was discovered by accident as the casks were originally taken on board as a convenient form of ballast.

In 1735 Hunt Roope opened lodges for wine in Vila Nova de Gaia and for fish in Viana. The ships of their fleet had some stirring adventures during those troublesome times. The brig *Jenny,* for instance, carrying Port to London, beat off a French privateer of eighteen guns. This achievement is depicted on the blue Portuguese tiles on the wall of the *lagar* at the Newman family *quinta,* Eira Velha.

The famous frigate duel in 1813 between H.M.S. *Shannon* and U.S.S. *Chesapeake* was the reason for the firm's Newfoundland House, Newman & Co. being allowed to fly the White Ensign at their offices. This unique honour was conferred by the Admiralty because twenty boys from the firm's brig *Duck* were pressed into service in the *Shannon* before the battle, and acquitted themselves magnificently.

At the beginning of this century the firm's Oporto interests were in the hands of a fabulous character, Cabel Roope, of whom many stories are told. Most, however, require some knowledge of Portuguese to be at all intelligible!

Roope had bought the great Eira Velha *quinta* for the company.

When the firm was sold to Ferreira in 1956, the *quinta* was bought by the Newman brothers, Sir Ralph and Tom Newman. Tom's son, Peter, now takes a great part in the running of the *quinta*, which is managed by the retired Cockburn director, Felix Vigne.

C. N. KOPKE & CO.   In 1636 Nicholas Kopke went to Lisbon as Consul for the Hanseatic towns, and settled permanently in Portugal. His son Christiano Kopke went up to Oporto in 1638, where he established himself as a general merchant, wine included.

The last direct descendant, Joaquim Kopke, died in 1895, already having sold his brand and business to the London Agents Mason Cattley & Co. in 1870. The firm in Oporto is now part of the Barros Almeida empire. In the last century Kopke shipped the wines of the famous Quinta de Roriz.

MACKENZIE, DRISCOLL & CO.   The firm was founded by Kenneth Mackenzie from Cadiz, hitherto well known as a sherry shipper, and in 1870 W. M. Driscoll, who had formerly been with Sandeman, was admitted into partnership. Though small, the house has always been well known for the quality of its wines, and it continued in the hands of the Mackenzie family until the post-war difficulties of the Port trade caused it to be sold to Ferreira.

I had the privilege and pleasure of working with Eric Mackenzie, the great-great-nephew of the founder, in the last years of my career.

MARTINEZ GASSIOT & CO. LTD.   This fine old firm was founded in 1797 by a Spaniard, D. Sebastian Gonzalez Martinez, who sold sherry, cigars and Port in London from an office in Mincing Lane. At that time the firm had no establishment in Portugal.

Mr. Martinez was joined by John Peter Gassiot in 1822, the style then being Martinez, Jones & Gassiot, though Jones soon faded from the scene leaving the title as it is to this day. In 1834 a lodge was taken in Vila Nova de Gaia, the manager from 1841 to 1881 being John F. Delaforce, the founder of the Delaforce dynasty in Oporto.

Mr. Martinez retired from the business in 1849, leaving J. P. Gassiot with his two sons John Peter Jnr. and Charles as the partners. The Gassiots were a remarkable and gifted family. J. P. Gassiot Snr. was a distinguished scientist and a great friend of

The maturing of Wood Port

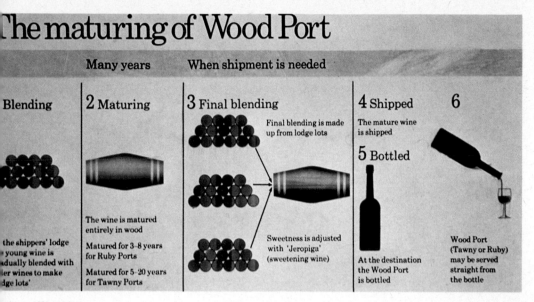

Many years   **When shipment is needed**

Blending

at the shippers' lodge
the young wine is
gradually blended with
other wines to make
lodge lots'

2 Maturing

The wine is matured
entirely in wood

Matured for 3-8 years
for Ruby Ports

Matured for 5-20 years
for Tawny Ports

3 Final blending

Final blending is made
up from lodge lots

Sweetness is adjusted
with 'Jeropiga'
(sweetening wine)

4 Shipped

The mature wine
is shipped

5 Bottled

At the destination
the Wood Port
is bottled

6

Wood Port
(Tawny or Ruby)
may be served
straight from
the bottle

A buyer selecting wines at the *quinta*

Interior of the Factory House, Oporto

Vila Nova de Gaia with some of its lodges

Faraday. He was at one time a vice-president of the Royal Society.

Charles Gassiot was a great patron of the arts, frequently buying the picture of the year at the Royal Academy. On his death he left a magnificent collection of paintings, chiefly to the City of London. He was a governor of St. Thomas's Hospital from 1871 until he died in 1902, and it was through his benefaction that a nurses' home, Gassiot House, was built in 1906. Because of rebuilding, it was demolished and a new Gassiot House, incorporating accommodation for 350 staff and the Nightingale School was opened in 1972. Charles Gassiot left the residue of his property in trust for the hospital, which on the final payment in 1936 realised £477,116. A plaque to his memory is in the hospital.

J. P. Gassiot Snr. retired about 1870. J. P. Gassiot Jnr. quarrelled with his brother Charles soon after, left the firm and never spoke to him again. J. P. Gassiot Jnr. left a portrait of Sebastian Martinez to the Vintners' Company, together with £4,000 for its installation and upkeep. The picture now hangs in the Vintners' Common Hall.

Charles took in as a partner his younger brother Commander Sebastian Gassiot, who left the navy to join him. Both Gassiots died in 1902 leaving no children. The executors then decided to float the firm as a public company, T. R. Harley becoming Managing Director. The old offices at Harp Lane were destroyed by incendiary bombs in 1940, and a move was made to 16 Mark Lane, only for these premises to be destroyed in turn. Fortunately a new home was found at 21 Harp Lane, the cellars running under the old house of London's famous Lord Mayor, Sir Richard Whittington, known as Dick Whittington.

On Harley's death in 1948, Geoffrey Beresford Smith, who had spent the war at sea in the navy, became Managing Director, a position he held until the sale of the company to Harvey's in 1961. I was privileged to have Geoffrey, already a friend of long-standing, as a close and very valued colleague until his retirement in 1971.

Martinez and Cockburn were always the keenest of rivals, and it is with a certain irony of fate that they now find themselves colleagues under the same umbrella. Geoffrey Beresford Smith has told me that he has seen a letter in their Oporto partners' office in which, during the 1830s, Cockburn had a lien on up to 500 pipes of Martinez' stock. On the face of it this would seem not unlikely, as Cockburn had not been in existence long and the ability to call on a quantity of fine quality wine would have been a very helpful insurance. Unfortunately like many records, the letter has disappeared. He also told me that in the 1870s and 1880s Cockburn, particularly in London, made the startling innovation of offering a special allowance of £4 per pipe for orders of ten pipes or more. Charles Gassiot resolutely refused to entertain such an absurd idea, to the considerable benefit of Cockburn, who obtained not a few new customers from Martinez.

To illustrate the overwhelming supremacy of fortified wines in the old days, Martinez Gassiot shipped more Port and sherry to the U.K. in the 1850s than any other firm in the trade.

A story from the Cockburn side is told by Gerald Cobb. Apparently, when Martinez went public, it was suggested to J. L. Teage that he might go over to London from Oporto to see if there could be any link up for Cockburn with a firm holding such a wonderful stock of old Port. His reason for inactivity was that he was too busy supervising repairs to the roof of the lodge. As an excuse it seems incredible.

MORGAN BROS.   *see* CROFT & CO.

NIEPOORT & CO.   The Niepoort's originally came from Holland. The firm is still independent and still controlled by the family.

OFFLEY FORRESTER LTD.   The firm was founded in 1761 under the style of Etty, Offley & Co. There is no record of an Offley ever residing in Oporto. Under its present title, it enshrines the name of unquestionably the greatest character, indeed genius is probably not too strong a description, ever produced by the Port trade, Joseph James Forrester.

The Forrester family came from Hull, the first being James in 1803, uncle of the great Joseph James, Barão de Forrester in the nobility of Portugal. J. J. Forrester adorned everything to which he turned his hand, and his versatility was remarkable. His greatest work was in connection with the production of Port, but in an insular age he learnt to speak Portuguese fluently and made a point of cultivating all classes of Portuguese society. He produced various maps, one of the whole length of the Douro from the Spanish frontier, another of the wine district, and another of the geological formation of the river and of the incidence of *oïdium tuckeri,* a virulent disease of the vines in the 1850s. He became the acknowledged expert on this disease, and it was for his many services to wine that his barony was conferred as well as many other international honours. Apart from these attainments he was also an artist and writer. His painting of wine shippers discussing their affairs in front of the Factory House in the Rua Nova dos Ingleses (now Rua Dom Infante Henrique) has been reproduced innumerable times.

In 1844, then still only thirty-three, Forrester published his pamphlet *A Word or Two on Port Wine,* in which he accused the whole trade of adulterating the wine, and coupled his allegations with a plea for the return of 'natural' Port; in other words, that the wine should not be made with the fermentation stopped by the addition of wine brandy, retaining some unfermented sugar (as Port has, in fact, been made since about that date). The battle was well and truly joined and, though most of the shippers very naturally took issue with Forrester, he had his supporters, particularly amongst the Portuguese firms.

Gradually the dust of controversy settled. Any malpractices there may have been disappeared, and it was fortunate indeed for the future of the trade that Forrester's plea for 'natural' wine went unheeded, since the result would have been a dry and rather harsh wine, not at all to the British taste. As it was, the Port trade was about to enter the period of its greatest prosperity.

In 1862 Forrester was drowned in dramatic circumstances in the river he loved so well. Accompanied by Dona Antonia Ferreira and Baroness Fladgate, his boat overturned in the dreaded rapids of the Cachão da Valeira. The ladies floated to safety in their crinolines, but Forrester's body was never found. He was wearing a belt full of gold sovereigns, normal practice in those days for paying the farmers, and is said to have remarked as they entered the gorge that the rudder was lashed the wrong way. No one will ever know whether it was accident or foul play. His son, William, was told that his father's body was found very early one morning at Pinhão, the money-belt removed and the body then sunk, which contradicts the official version that his body was never found.

One of the older English vices, that of litigation, led to difficulties for the firm, and in 1908 a complete reconstruction was found necessary. In 1962 it was incorporated in the Sandeman Group, who, in 1965, sold 50% of the firm to the St. Raphael Company of

France. Offley Vintages have been traditionally largely based on the wines of the famous Quinta Boa Vista.

QUARLES HARRIS & CO.   Founded in 1680, the firm is one of the oldest, and the Harris family has one of the longest connections with the British colony in Oporto. In the course of time through family relationships the firm became absorbed by the two Houses of Noble & Murat and Warre & Co., the wines being shipped by the latter under the Quarles Harris Brand.

In the early 1920s the firm was reconstituted by A. J. Symington and Reginald Quarles Harris, and is now owned by the Symington family. I remember Mr. Reginald Harris when I first went to Oporto, a distinguished if diminutive figure, always immaculately turned out and wearing an old-fashioned trimmed imperial beard.

RAMOS PINTO, ADRIANO   One of the leading Portuguese houses, they own the beautiful Quinta Bom Retiro in the Rio Torto Valley. Originally their trade was principally to Brazil, but is now evenly spread in a number of markets. Their Managing Director is Senhor José Antonio Rosas to whom I am so vastly indebted for facts and figures.

ROBERTSON BROS. & CO.   Formerly owners of the well-known Quinta Roncão, Robertson's Vintage wine was shipped under the brand Rebello Valente (originally belonging to Allen & Co.), bought by Robertson's many years ago. Robertson Bros. themselves were sold in 1953 to Sandeman, who did not however buy Quinta Roncão.

THE ROYAL OPORTO WINE CO. – COMPANHIA GERAL DA AGRICULTURA DOS VINHOS DO ALTO DOURO   Also known in Portugal as Companhia Velha, the 'Old Company'. This was the monopoly company founded in 1756 by Royal Decree on the advice of the First Minister, the Marquis de Pombal.

From 1756 until 1827 the company enjoyed the privileges of a monopolist position, much resented by the rest of the trade, although a considerable amount of research and improvement in the field of viticulture was undertaken. Eventually the trade was able to show that the abuses of the system outweighed the benefits.

In 1843 a new company was set up under the old name, but trading as conventional shippers. After the last war the firm came into the Real Companhia Vinicola Group owned by the meteoric tycoon Senhor da Silva Reis. The company has lately come again under government control, but, needless to say, without any of its former powers.

ROZES, ED. A French company now owned by Domecq. The Gaia Company is a joint venture between Domecq and Taylor.

SANDEMAN, GEORGE G. & CO. LTD. In 1790 a Scottish gentleman of Perth, George Sandeman, founded in London, with a loan of £300 from his father, the great firm which bears his name. Until 1796 David Sandeman was in partnership with his brother, but by 1798 the partnership had been amicably dissolved, and David devoted his energies to founding the Commercial Bank of Scotland.

George Sandeman soon extended his interests to Oporto, and this happily coincided with the great flowering of the Port trade at the start of the nineteenth century, a succession of fine Vintages being made popular by Wellington's officers in the Peninsular War. In 1805 the London offices were transferred to 20 St. Swithin's Lane, which remained until recently the firm's headquarters.

George Sandeman was succeeded by his nephew G. G. Sandeman, who in turn took his eldest son, A. G. Sandeman, into partnership. A. G. Sandeman's three brothers also joined the firm, one of them Colonel J. G. Sandeman, who took part as a subaltern of the 1st Royal Dragoons in the charge of the Heavy Brigade at Balaclava.

The firm is now a public company, but the two senior directors are T. W. and D. P. Sandeman, in the direct family line.

In 1922, Sandeman launched what might be described as the first modern marketing campaign by deciding to offer their wines in bottle only and bearing the Sandeman label. This was an act of great courage, for overnight they lost most of their traditional market. Their example has since been widely followed!

Tim Sandeman tells me that the firm first started advertising in India in 1909, then in other countries and in 1913 in England. He also quoted a charming rhyme used in the 1930s in Ireland, where Sandeman's are particularly strong.

There was a young girl from Clonmel,
Who was anaemic and not at all well,
The doctor she sought prescribed Sandeman's Port,
And now she's as sound as a bell.

As befits a firm of their standing, Sandeman have been fortunate in having a line of distinguished Oporto managers, the last three being Hubert and Gwyn Jennings, father and son, with Lacey Rumsey holding the reins in between.

A. J. DA SILVA & CO.   This well-known house was founded in 1813 by Senhor José Antonio da Silva, remaining entirely in the hands of the da Silva family until 1920. Senhor A. J. da Silva Jnr. and Dona Theresa da Silva then brought into partnership Senhor da Silva's son-in-law, Senhor Luiz Vasconcellos Porto and his wife, Senhor da Silva's only daughter.

It was Luiz Porto who developed the magnificent Quinta do Noval into one of the great show places of the Douro, and he was the first to experiment with the wide, gradually-sloping terraces for the vines instead of the old narrow ones, so expensive to construct and maintain. He was succeeded by his two grandsons, the van Zeller brothers, of whom Dr. Fernando van Zeller has had a particularly distinguished career in the trade organisation in Oporto. Since 1908 all A. J. da Silva Vintages have been shipped as Noval.

SILVA & COSENS   This firm owes its origin to Senhor Bruno Avaristo Ferrerira da Silva, a Portuguese gentleman from Oporto, who came to England in 1798 to sell Port, married an English lady and settled there. He died in 1850, being succeeded by his son J. J. da Silva, who founded the firm in 1862. He was succeeded in turn by his son Edward, who was joined by F. W. Cosens.

In 1868 a member of the Warre family first became a partner, followed in 1877 by James Ramsay Dow, whose firm Dow & Co. was merged with Silva & Cosens, and whose name is perpetuated in the Vintage brand.

Mr. Dow was a Victorian 'character'. It is said of him that, when calling on a country wine merchant to obtain business, he was twice told that the gentleman concerned was out. Going back a third time he saw through the window the merchant seated at his desk. Determined not to be thwarted, Dow rang the bell, put his foot in the door and marched into the office. Seizing the key he locked the door on the outside and departed without a word, throwing the key into a nearby canal. History relates that he came back a week later and obtained the order.

In 1912 the firm became virtually amalgamated with Warre &

Co., and with the departure of Amyas Warre to run the London office, both firms were managed in Oporto by A. J. Symington, who had joined Warre's in 1905. Symington was the first of the clan who now take such a large and active part in the Port trade and in the affairs of the British community in general. The family own the Quinta do Bomfim at Pinhão, and their offices in Gaia are in the house previously lived in by J. J. Forrester.

SMITH WOODHOUSE & CO.   This firm was founded in 1784 by Christopher Smith, who at the age of seventy-seven had the distinction of becoming Lord Mayor of London in 1817. He was joined by the Woodhouse brothers in 1818, Robert the younger marrying a Miss Pinto Basto of the well-known Portuguese family.

The firm was carried on for many years in Oporto by the Woodhouse family, and then by Mr. Flude, who, for over sixty years, was connected with the firm in various capacities. The brand 'Smith Woodhouse' was bought by Luis Gordon & Sons Ltd. of London in 1956, and their wines were shipped by W. J. Graham & Co., now part of the Silva & Cosens Group. In the 1960s Graham also acquired the brand name, thus becoming the complete owners.

TAYLOR FLADGATE & YEATMAN   This great house, especially renowned for their vintage wines, goes back to 1692 under the title of Job Bearsley of Viana. Bearsley's son Peter was the first Englishman to penetrate the Alto Douro for the purpose of buying wine, and his brother Bartholomew bought the first known British property in the Douro, the Casa dos Alambiques, near Régua, which Taylor's still own.

The Casa dos Alambiques played its part in the Peninsular War when it was used as a field hospital by the British army and their Portuguese allies.

The Bearsley family was connected with the firm right up to 1806, and in 1808, very sensibly in view of the French threat of invasion, Mr. Camo, the only American ever to be made a partner in an Oporto shipping house, joined the firm. As a neutral Mr. Camo was able to render yeoman service in preserving not only his own stocks, but also to a great extent those of his colleagues as well; but even he felt it prudent to retire to Lisbon on Marshal Soult's approach in 1809, only to return three weeks later when Wellington recaptured Oporto. Mr. Camo disappears from the firm's annals in 1812, when the Americans declared war on England.

The first Taylor came into the firm in 1816, the first Fladgate in 1837 and the first Yeatman in 1844, since which date the style has remained unaltered.

In 1899 the partners were C. N. Skeffington and the two brothers, Harry and Frank Yeatman. Skeffington died in 1901, and Harry Yeatman in 1921; Harry Yeatman's son, Julian was the co-author of the classic *1066 and All That*.

Frank Yeatman remained as the sole proprietor until joined by his son Dick in 1924, and by his nephew Stanley Yeatman in 1927. Frank was among the great characters of the trade, and with Archie Smithes of Cockburn was generally considered to be one of the two greatest judges of Port.

After the war the firm suffered grievous blows through the deaths not only of Frank Yeatman at a great age and much revered, but also of Colin Yeatman, Stanley's nephew, killed in a tragic accident at the Oporto British Club, Stanley himself at the early age of fifty-five, and finally of Dick Yeatman.

The firm is now run by Dick's nephew, Alastair Robertson, Huyshe Bower, a cousin, Bruce Guimaraens (who chiefly looks after the firm of his name) and Jeremy Bull. They own the famous Quinta de Vargellas bought in 1894, and in 1973 acquired a further two *quintas* in the Alto Douro, both of which had supplied wines for Taylor's Vintages since early in the last century. Taylor continue to have the highest reputation for their Vintage Ports, which consistently fetch the best prices at London auctions.

WARRE & CO. The earliest recorded member of this great firm was John Clark, whose marriage was registered at the Oporto Factory in 1718. It is, however, certain that the firm was in existence before this date, as Warre's are known to have been shipping wine through Viana and, in fact, kept an office there, importing *bacalhau* under the style of C. H. Noble & Murat, right up to 1894.

The first Warre entered the business in 1729, and married a sister of Consul Whitehead, the builder of the Factory House. William Warre, born in Oporto in 1784, was A.D.C. to Lord Beresford during the Peninsular War, and eventually rose to Lieutenant-General. He had always wanted to be a soldier, but as a boy was put to work in the family business. One hot afternoon in the office in the Rua Nova dos Ingleses, Pedro Alves, a Portuguese member of the firm, fell asleep at his desk. The opportunity was too good to miss. William fixed the sleeper's pigtail to the desk with sealing-wax. A monumental row resulted, and William achieved his ambition to be sent for a soldier.

In 1905 the surviving partner, Robert Stuart, requiring assistance to run the firm, was joined by A. J. Symington, who after starting his career with Graham's had for some years been manager of Southard's, including the period covered by the Burnay sale. In 1912 Stuart retired and Symington took in as partners, G. F. Warre, Amyas F. Warre and E. D. Lawson. With the Warres concentrating on the London end of the business, A. J. Symington's sons and grandsons have managed the shipping side with great success, and continue to do so.

In 1965, with the growth of business in France, Warre's agents there, Dubonnet-Cinzano-Byrrh, were admitted into partnership.

WIESE & KROHN   Of German origin. This small company is still independent, shipping to many markets under the direction of Senhor Fernando Carneiro.

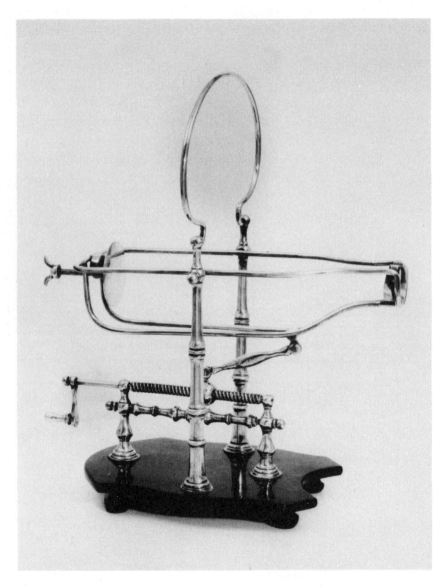

A decanting cradle *circa* 1900. Mounted on a wooden base, the elevated parts in electro-plated silver, with a carrying handle at the top, the bottle cradle fitted on each side to a column, with an adjustable plate to allow for the exact size of bottle. The angle of the cradle can be adjusted by a handle controlling a threaded horizontal bar, to which the cradle is hinged.

Reminiscences

The offices of Cockburn Smithes & Co., 60 Mark Lane in the City of London, were in January 1930, if not Victorian, certainly Edwardian in character; as indeed was most of the City in the region of Tower Hill, Mark Lane itself, Mincing Lane, Great Tower Street, Eastcheap and a host of other lanes and alleys, the centre of the wine and corn trade. 'London Particulars' were by no means uncommon; the old phrase "I could not see my hand before my face" was almost literally true in the thick yellow fog that could last all day during the winter months.

In the streets there was almost as much horse-drawn traffic as there were motor cars with all the attendant mess and slush. Everyone from the newest-joined office boy wore heavy dark suits, winter and summer, with bowler hat, umbrella and, of course, hair cut 'short back and sides'. Time in the present day sense meant nothing. It was almost impossible to walk down the street in E.C.3 without meeting a trade acquaintance and the man whose office was nearest would, almost as a matter of course, ask the other in for a drink. "Have a glass of wine, my boy" meant in those days a glass of old Tawny Port (dry White Port had not been invented), and more often than not this meant a good deal more than one glass.

The office furnishing was Victorian in the extreme, high stools and desks, loose boxes for the senior staff in the main office and behind a swing door more loose-boxes for the partners adjoining the lunch room and sample room.

The office staff was large, some eight men – from the manager, a venerable old gentleman nearing retirement, to myself, then the office junior – one girl secretary and two cellarmen. There were two partners in London, Ernest Cockburn, who actually hired me and behind whose desk I have sat for many years, his cousin Fred Cockburn and two salaried directors, my cousin Colin Gordon and Captain Frank Ree retired from the navy. Office hours were from 9.30 a.m. 'until the work was finished' which, with luck, often meant 5 p.m. in the summer. The Board always lunched in the office. It was usually a reasonably quick affair, but if customers were being entertained it was quite likely that the Port would still be going round at 6.30 p.m.

Letters were copied in a letter-press with damp sheets, and were usually illegible either because the sheets were too dry or too damp, when everything was smudged. All invoices were written by hand and in great detail with everything such as insurance, freight etc. being itemised, and the final phrase 'Delivered by Murray & Laker's van' frequently referring to a horse-drawn vehicle. The

'It's very strong,' said Miss Pole, as she put down her glass; 'I do believe there is spirit in it.'

Cranford by Mrs. Gaskell

dock clerk made a daily trip on foot to the London docks, where many hundreds of pipes of Port were held as bonded stock, to lodge the necessary papers to clear any wine that had been ordered. While in the docks it was considered necessary to taste a sample from one or two casks to see if all was well and, curiously enough, the ones selected were always the best so that the ullage of some pipes on clearance was rather more than might have been expected. For the unwary emerging from the cool vaults with two or three glasses of Old Tawny on board into a hot summer's day with blazing heat reflected from the cobbles, the result could be disastrous. On more than one occasion I found it prudent to walk from the docks near Tower Bridge to my digs in Maida Vale and I still felt very peculiar on arrival.

There was generally a more free and easy attitude towards drinking in those days. Duty free, dock bottle (24 ounce), landing samples of every cask of the hundreds shipped to London were kept for three months in a special room next to the cellar and it was often customary for the staff to gather at the end of the lunch break to take a glass or two from one of the higher quality wines. In fact the old bookkeeper was usually sound asleep from about 2.30 p.m. onwards and if woken up did not make much sense. When, as sometimes happened, he was summoned to answer some question or other by one of the partners the excuse was always "Mr. X has just gone out to buy some cigarettes". The matter was never pressed.

The sample room was a great centre of activity before the war. Standardisation of marks was minimal although stocks of standard marks of various qualities were kept in bond in London for quick delivery and to get 'landing age'. But the great part of our business was in many hundreds of customers' private marks often with only very small differences from standard blends. In order to make up samples of these marks from the marks book (still in existence), sample bottles of the Oporto lodge lots were kept in racks and it was the duty of the sample clerk to keep these up to date and to re-order as necessary from Portugal. From every cask shipped to London a landing sample was drawn which had to be tasted and passed by a partner, sometimes as many as a hundred at a time. The sample clerk was then responsible for storing the samples (and for stopping the rest of the staff drinking the important ones).

The real test was in matching samples of other shippers' wines, as requested by a merchant, and our London office always tried to find a match unless the type of wine was so unusual that the only solution was to send it out to Oporto. For the purpose of matching, thirty or so lodge lots of various styles, colours and qualities were used as the basic range from which to blend, and though this highly-skilled tasting was always done by a partner, the sample clerk would often be asked his opinion before final approval of the sample, which he would then make up for despatch entering full details of the blend in the sample book.

This tasting and matching was to me, the real fascination of the trade, in which one's professional skill was put to the test. It was, in fact, the only true training in my profession I ever received in the old firm. Such knowledge of business that I have eventually picked up came much later.

On days when there were long lunches 'inside', the actual work would be finished by about 5 p.m. and the time had to be passed somehow until we could go home. Climbing round the room without touching the floor was popular, leading to terrible clattering falls, and shooting at the letter-press with an air pistol leading to terrifying ricochets was also in vogue; or we would go down to the cellar and play ping-pong on the bottling board. When the lunch was finally over there would be a concerted rush to the lunch room as soon as the coast was clear to finish up any food or wine. We were not overpaid (I started at £7 per month), even allowing for the very different value of money in those days, and any augmentation of our meagre lunch was very welcome.

The cellar was really a private luxury in those days. It was filled with bins of Vintage Port, used entirely for lunch-room entertaining, partners' private reserves, two or three hogsheads of 'CF' (now called Directors' Reserve) ready for bottling and used for day-to-day drinking, and a considerable quantity of various clarets all bought from Rutherford Osborne & Perkin (who had succeeded us as agents for Cruse in 1899). Again this claret was drunk exclusively by the partners. The staff were not supposed to drink CF, but a hogshead of lower quality, though still Fine Tawny, was kept bottled for us.

One of the curiosities of those days is that, though Port as a whole was still the largest single wine imported, Vintage Port was very much in the doldrums. Although prices were ridiculously low, even by standards then, and a bottle would cost around 5/- to 8/-, the type of person drinking Vintage had been particularly hard hit by the economic slump. Drinking Vintage meant decanting and handling problems, and no one could afford butlers and parlourmaids anymore. The cost of Cockburn's 1927 standing in customers' books was about 42/- per dozen duty paid, and I remember getting back from France in 1940 and being shown the Army & Navy Stores' summer list for that year, when the leading '27s were still quoted at 6/- per bottle, full retail price. Prices did, however, begin to move upwards shortly afterwards.

One of my duties as office boy was to man a primitive telephone switchboard and, in order to try and learn something of the business, I used to listen in eagerly to conversations. One day in the very early '30s, an extremely distinguished West End wine merchant who had been allocated two pipes of 1927, rang up and asked to speak to Ernest Cockburn. "Is that you Ernest?", he said. "That 1927 of yours is so light, my boy, it tastes like breakfast wine. Will you take it back?". "Yes of course". Not bad breakfast wine at 42/– a dozen as those who have tasted it will agree. It now fetches, when available, well over £200 a case.

'Port?' asked Mrs. Markham.
'Port in course,' replied Mr. J. . . 'give me a good fruity wine; with a grip o' the gob that leaves a mark on the side o' the glass . . .'

Mr. Jorrocks – Handley Cross by R. S. Surtees

Our business was entirely confined to selling Cockburn's Port in bulk, and any talk of labels was complete anathema. "We appeal to the customer with the quality of our wines" was the cry, and any customer who wanted to incorporate the name Cockburn on his label had to submit a sketch for our approval, and, of course, print the label at his own expense.

Looking back, I am struck by the firm's great confidence. Although, with the benefit of hindsight, it is obvious that the Port trade was at best static, the prestige of Port and of Cockburn's in particular was so great that, in the partners' opinion, the rest of the trade hardly existed, though sherry, coming up fast, was regarded as a foe worthy of their steel. It is worth remembering that in those days, high-strength sweet red wines ruled the roost. They included Port, large quantities of Australian, South African (before their 'sherry' became so highly regarded) and British wine almost all sweet red. The quantity of unfortified wine cleared was relatively small.

After three and a half years working my way occupying all the 'seats' in the office except that of bookkeeping, which was sacrosanct, I was sent to Oporto in the summer of 1933 to do my year there and to learn as much as possible about Port. My salary was now £108 a year, my digs were paid for by the firm and I can with certainty say I have never been so well off since. Living was dirt cheap, entertaining was regal and sport at the British Club cost nothing.

I returned to London in the summer of 1934 and the next step, which meant that I had really scaled Olympus, was to go on the road for the firm. I was summoned before the four directors (the partnership had become a private unlimited company in 1931) and told the great news that I was to 'travel'. Making suitably gratified noises at the honour, but also greatly daring, I asked how selling Cockburn's Port was actually done. The question was greeted with a stunned silence; it had obviously never been asked before and I had clearly made a terrible gaffe. After a prolonged pause someone said "Have you got a bowler hat?" This was a stupid question, since had I not had one I would not have been allowed in the office at all. Somebody else said "Well, never mention Cockburn's Port". Had anyone present known the phrase then, this was the original 'softsell' and made good sense. We only sold Cockburn's Port in bulk, there was no price list, and it was pretty obvious to the dimmest country wine merchant what a young man presenting Cockburn Smithes & Company's card was there for. Later, gaining experience, I learnt to modify my instructions somewhat. After spending hours talking on everything under the sun and never mentioning the forbidden subject, I would occasionally whisper as I left "May we ship you another pipe?".

Most travelling was still by train, as calling by car was considered 'infra dig'. If one did use a car it had to be left round the corner out of sight, so that one could pretend to have come specially to that town by train.

I had a large number of London, as well as country, customers to look after, and in addition a good deal of sample-room work in tasting and matching samples. When I first came back from Oporto, filled with the enthusiasm of youth and thinking I knew it all, I must have been a sore trial to my colleagues. Frank Ree and I used to taste a lot together, having similar palates, and one day after I had been particularly abrasive, he said that he had a specially important piece of tasting for me; would I taste four wines 'blind', writing down my findings so that he could study them? Taking a long time and enormous care, I noted that one wine was a little drier, one a little better quality, one a little darker than the others and so on, and eventually took my findings into Frank. Putting his glasses on the end of his nose, he studied the rigmarole with great care. At last, looking up he said, "Wyndham, I congratulate you – a masterpiece, but I should tell you that all those wines were out of the same bottle!" It was a lesson I have never forgotten.

'I cherish the fact that Port speaks the sentences of wisdom, Burgundy sings the inspired Ode.'

Rev. Dr. Middleton – The Egoist by George Meredith

One success I had as a traveller shows the spirit of the trade and times. We had reason to believe that a small German wine shipper occasionally bought a little Port, and as we had in bond a quarter cask of a mark that was sticking, I thought I would try my luck. Three hours and four bottles of the shipper's Moselle later the quarter cask was sold with mutual back-slapping. The son of the shipper concerned , who afterwards became a great friend and who told me the story many years later, said to his father, "Why on earth did you buy that cask of Port – we don't want it?"; "No, of course not my boy, but he was such a nice young man!"

The 1930s rolled on and trade in general, under the influence of rearmament, started to pick up after the 1931 slump. The 1935 Vintage was offered in 1937, but interest was very patchy. Half the trade had already offered the 1934s and stocks of older Vintage Port were enormous. Little did we know that within four or five years most of this wine would either be bombed out of existence or disgorged and drunk as Wood Port, in default of anything else available.

In 1938, when war loomed ahead, I thought it prudent to get in on the act so I joined the Territorial Army. By 1939, my salary at £480 a year, I was allowed to lunch in the Wine Trade Club at the firm's expense, but never, of course, in the Directors' office lunchroom. That August, in an extraordinary atmosphere of expectancy, half dread, the Wine Trade Club was shut as usual for the holidays and we were accommodated in the now defunct City Carlton Club. On 24 August a wine trade friend, in the same Territorial Regiment as myself, was lunching with me there and we were enjoying a postprandial glass of Port. By that date no Territorial Officer could be out of his office without leaving a telephone number. At 2.45 p.m. the telephone call came. Deciding the German army would wait, we had another glass of Port and a cigar and then went off to war.

My only other sight of the office until December 1945 was from Primrose Hill, to watch it burn, together with many other buildings in the City of London. This was the first fire raid of Christmas 1940. The office building was extensively damaged but the cellar remained intact. 60 Mark Lane was finally destroyed in the great raid of May 1941, though again providentially the cellar more or less escaped.

In 1941, when it seemed likely that Hitler would invade Portugal, Cockburn shipped a thousand pipes of Port to their American agent in New York. These wines represented all our basic brands so that if the worst happened we should have stocks on which to build again. Shortly before the end of the war, we were lucky enough to find new offices in the City of London, at 33 Eastcheap, with the truncated cellar in Mark Lane still usable. There had been small, though very irregular shipments from Portugal throughout the war, and with great good fortune our bonded stocks were not destroyed so that we were able to keep our regular customers going on very small quotas.

From the beginning of 1944 the Government Quota Scheme handled by the Port Wine Trade Association was in operation.

Quotas were based on shipments in 1939 and the amounts were very small, frequently only a few bottles, but better than nothing. These quotas were the cause of an immensely important and unforeseen development. Before that time bottles of Port were seldom labelled by the shipper. Now the system required some identifying mark on the bottle and the first Cockburn label was therefore designed. When things got back to normal these labels were supplied for wine in bulk, and thereby the foundation of Cockburn's as a brand was well and truly laid.

Fred Cockburn, Frank Ree and I were all demobilised at the end of 1945, with Colin Gordon and the rest of the staff returning one by one. The last back was Frank Bayley, the Manager who, as the oldest of us, had taken the rump of the office from London up to our Scottish agents, Robertson & Baxter in Glasgow. He was not called up for the R.A.F. until 1942, then found himself beseiged by the Japanese in Kohima. We were lucky enough not to have any fatal casualties in the firm, though John Gladwin with the Green Jackets was wounded in North Africa and I had a tooth knocked out by a stone thrown up by a tank track in Normandy!

The new office was extremely old-fashioned, electricity and gas were in short supply and there was very little coal to be had. The first two winters of peace were bitterly cold; there was no new business; our quotas were allocated as they came in, and calling on wine merchants was therefore a formality and kept to a minimum. We spent our time examining stock; in other words tasting through our old Vintage Ports and other wines. Astonishingly, in view of the rough treatment, very few of the bins had suffered in any way at all.

Gradually the clouds began to lift. Quite unexpectedly, import quotas for Port were removed in the autumn of 1949, and we were able to go out and get new business, flaunting our new labels. The Korean war gave a welcome fillip to Port shipments, since the fear of a general conflagration caused importers to build up stocks against this event, but not unfortunately to consumption. Trade remained static at a low level. We offered and shipped the 1947 Vintage (still under quota), the 1950, 1955 and 1960, all of which helped but did not cure the general malaise in the trade. In the early 1950s, after the gravest deliberations, we decided to offer Cockburn's Port in bottle to supplement our bulk trade. This quickly grew to a sizeable turnover by the standards of those days, without having any effect on our cask sales. But still costs rose, prices were too low and because of this turnover grew too slowly and capital was short.

With the greatest reluctance the old family business decided the time had come for the tune to be played by another orchestra. To mix the metaphor, we put our money on the right horse which is now certainly leading the field. John Harvey & Sons of Bristol, who had been one of our most important customers for many years, acquired the business.

'Wal'r, my boy,' replied the Captain, 'in the Proverbs of Solomon you will find the following words, "May we never want a friend in need, nor a bottle to give him!" When found, make a note of.'

Captain Cuttle – Dombey & Son by Charles Dickens

It is well known that Port is usually the drink for the loyal toast and also that in the Royal Navy it is drunk seated. Sarah Bradford says that it was George III who on standing to honour the loyal toast bumped his head on the low deck-head above, but I have always understood that it was William IV, 'Silly Billy', who had served in the navy and who suffered in this way. Anyhow, there is no doubt that a royal cranium took a knock, and the edict to the Royal Navy went forth that the toast should be drunk safely seated.

In the army the drinking of Port probably came in more or less by accident, when claret was scarce due to the almost continual wars with France and thereby suffered the taint of being an unpatriotic wine. 'Disloyal' Jacobites too, were said to toast 'the King over the water' in claret.

Port, until recently, has always been considered the villain of the piece by sufferers from gout, and many excellent cartoons have given credence to this belief. Fortunately modern medical science has completely acquitted Port of the crime, and has proved that it is caused by an excess of uric acid in the blood brought on by stress. It is not hereditary, and teetotallers can – and do – suffer from gout.

'A pint of old Port and a devilled biscuit can hurt no man.'

Dr. Swizzle – Handley Cross by R. S. Surtees

There is no doubt, though, that excess of wine does cause uric acid, and when wine drinking was thought to be the sole cause of gout, Port was the 'fashionable' wine, drunk in enormous quantities by modern standards. Had the sufferers drunk the same amount of claret, sherry or any other wine, accompanied as this imbibing was by a vast consumption of rich food, especially red meat, the result would have been exactly the same. A. P. Herbert put it nicely in *Punch*:

*At last the happy truth is out
Port is not the cause of gout;
Far more responsible for pain,
Are kidneys, liver, sweetbread, brain.*

The clubman should by any means,
Avoid anchovies and sardines,
And citizens of every sort,
Owe some apology to Port!

Great play is often made in Britain about the correct way round the Port should go at table. This, combined with the barbaric convention, happily falling into disuse, that the ladies should leave the dining-room before the Port, utterly bewilders the unwary foreigner. Various myths have been thought up to explain why the Port is passed clockwise from right to left. The usual explanation is that this progression of the decanter leaves the sword-arm free for emergencies – though too bad for the left-handed!

'But leave the bottle on the chimney piece and let me put my lips to it when so dispoged.'
Mrs. Gamp – Martin Chuzzlewit by Charles Dickens

There are some catch phrases, usually connected with Bishops who neglected to pass the port, to warn those offenders who allow the decanter to linger too long in front of them. The one I like best is the naval 'It's a long ship'.

A word on bottle sizes, though now it is very rare to find Port bottled in anything bigger than a magnum as the bigger sizes of bottle are probably not made any more:

Two bottles – a Magnum

Three bottles – a Tappit-hen (in Scotland sometimes 'cock' as opposed to 'hen').

Four bottles – a Jeroboam

Six bottles – a Rehoboam.

Part of the mystique of wine is the way it is inextricably involved with the history of the country in which it is produced or in which it is usually drunk. Port is no exception and part of its appeal may lie subconsciously in its involvement with our greatest days as a nation. With hindsight we can say that Hitler was certainly much more of a menace than Napoleon, but in the very early years of the nineteenth century we stood alone against the threatening might of the Grande Armée, behind which was a cowed or conquered Europe. Roast beef, strong ale and Port was the Englishman's staple fare in those days. By 1815 this country stood at the pinnacle of power. May one dare to hope that a recovery from our present state could be helped by a return to this fare, even though strong ale may be difficult to find?

Appendix

Vintage Ports and their shippers from 1870 to 1975

This list refers to shippers' vintages offered to the United Kingdom and does not include years which were shipped to other countries only. It must also be pointed out that the various sources, including shippers themselves, do not always agree that a particular year was shipped, but when in doubt it has been included. The bottling of some of the older vintages took place anything between two and five years after the vintage.

Adams	1935, 1945, 1947, 1948, 1950, 1955, 1960, 1963, 1966
Barros Almeida	1943, 1975
Borges	1914, 1922, 1924, 1963
Burmester	1873, 1878, 1887, 1890, 1896, 1900, 1904, 1908, 1912, 1920, 1922, 1927, 1931, 1935, 1937, 1940, 1943, 1945, 1948, 1954, 1955, 1958, 1960, 1963
Butler Nephew	1922, 1924, 1927, 1934, 1942, 1945, 1947, 1948, 1955, 1957, 1958, 1960, 1975
Calem	1935, 1947, 1948, 1955, 1958, 1960, 1963, 1975
Cockburn	1870, 1872, 1873, 1875, 1878, 1881, 1884, 1887, 1890, 1894, 1896, 1900, 1904, 1908, 1912, 1927, 1935, 1947, 1950, 1955, 1960, 1963, 1967, 1970, 1975
Croft	1870, 1872, 1875, 1878, 1881, 1884, 1885, 1887, 1890, 1894, 1896, 1897, 1900, 1904, 1908, 1912, 1917, 1920, 1922, 1924, 1927, 1935, 1942, 1945, 1950, 1955, 1960, 1963, 1966, 1970, 1975
Da Silva, A. J., (Quinta do Noval)	1896, 1900, 1904, 1908, 1912, 1917, 1919, 1920, 1923, 1927, 1931, 1934, 1941, 1942, 1945, 1947, 1948, 1950, 1955, 1958, 1960, 1962, 1963, 1966, 1969, 1970, 1972, 1975
Delaforce	1870, 1873, 1875, 1878, 1881, 1884, 1887, 1890, 1894, 1896, 1900, 1904, 1908, 1912, 1917, 1919, 1920, 1927, 1935, 1945, 1947, 1950, 1955, 1958, 1960, 1963, 1966, 1970, 1975
Diez Hermanos	1975
Dixon	1884, 1887, 1890
Dow	1870, 1872, 1873, 1875, 1878, 1881, 1884,

	1887, 1890, 1892, 1896, 1899, 1904, 1908,
	1912, 1917, 1919, 1920, 1924, 1927, 1931,
	1934, 1935, 1945, 1947, 1950, 1955, 1960,
	1963, 1966, 1970, 1972, 1975
Feist	1922
Ferreira, A. A.	1894, 1896, 1897, 1900, 1904, 1908, 1912,
	1917, 1920, 1924, 1927, 1935, 1937
Ferreira, A. A., Sucrs.	1945, 1955, 1960, 1963, 1966, 1970, 1975
Feuerheerd	1870, 1872, 1873, 1875, 1878, 1881, 1884,
	1887, 1890, 1894, 1896, 1900, 1904, 1908,
	1912, 1917, 1920, 1924, 1927, 1942, 1943,
	1944, 1945, 1951, 1955, 1957, 1960, 1963,
	1966, 1970
Fonseca	1870, 1873, 1878, 1881, 1884, 1887, 1890,
	1896, 1900, 1904, 1908, 1912, 1920, 1922,
	1924, 1927, 1934, 1945, 1948, 1955, 1960,
	1963, 1966, 1970, 1975
Guimaraens	1958, 1961, 1962
Gonzalez Byass	1896, 1900, 1904, 1908, 1912, 1917, 1920,
	1945, 1955, 1960, 1963, 1967, 1970, 1975
Gould Campbell	1870, 1872, 1873, 1875, 1878, 1881, 1884,
	1885, 1887, 1890, 1892, 1896, 1900, 1904,
	1908, 1912, 1917, 1920, 1922, 1924, 1927,
	1934, 1942, 1955, 1960, 1963, 1966, 1975
Graham	1870, 1872, 1873, 1875, 1878, 1880, 1881,
	1884, 1885, 1887, 1890, 1892, 1894, 1896,
	1897, 1900, 1901, 1904, 1908, 1912, 1917,
	1920, 1924, 1927, 1935, 1942, 1945, 1948,
	1955, 1960, 1963, 1966, 1970, 1975
Kingston	1922, 1924, 1927
Kopke	1870, 1872, 1873, 1875, 1878, 1881, 1884,
	1887, 1890, 1892, 1894, 1896, 1897, 1900,
	1904, 1908, 1912, 1917, 1919, 1920, 1922,
	1927, 1935, 1945, 1948, 1950, 1952, 1955,
	1958, 1960, 1963, 1966, 1970
Mackenzie	1870, 1873, 1875, 1878, 1881, 1884, 1887,
	1890, 1896, 1900, 1904, 1908, 1912, 1919,
	1920, 1922, 1927, 1935, 1945, 1947, 1948,
	1950, 1952, 1954, 1955, 1957, 1958, 1960,
	1963, 1966
Martinez (Gassiot)	1870, 1872, 1873, 1874, 1875, 1878, 1880,
	1881, 1884, 1885, 1886, 1887, 1890, 1892,
	1894, 1896, 1897, 1900, 1904, 1908, 1911,
	1912, 1919, 1922, 1927, 1931, 1934, 1945,
	1955, 1958, 1960, 1963, 1967, 1970, 1975
Messias	1975

Morgan	1870, 1872, 1873, 1875, 1878, 1881, 1884, 1887, 1890, 1894, 1896, 1900, 1904, 1908, 1912, 1920, 1922, 1924, 1927, 1942, 1948, 1950, 1955, 1960, 1963, 1966
Niepoort	1927, 1945
Offley Forrester (Boa Vista)	1870, 1872, 1873, 1874, 1875, 1878, 1881, 1884, 1885, 1887, 1888, 1890, 1892, 1894, 1896, 1897, 1900, 1902, 1904, 1908, 1910, 1912, 1919, 1920, 1922, 1924, 1925, 1927, 1929, 1935, 1950, 1954, 1960, 1962, 1963, 1966, 1967, 1970, 1972, 1975
Quarles Harris	1927, 1934, 1945, 1947, 1950, 1955, 1958, 1960, 1963, 1966, 1975
Pinto dos Santos, A.,	1955, 1957, 1958, 1960, 1963, 1966, 1970, 1974, 1975
Manoel d'Porcas Jnr.	1967, 1975
Ramos Pinto	1924, 1927, 1945, 1955, 1970
Real Vinicola (Quinta do Sibio)	1945, 1947, 1950, 1955, 1960
Rebello Valente	1870, 1875, 1878, 1881, 1884, 1887, 1890, 1892, 1894, 1896, 1897, 1900, 1904, 1908, 1911, 1912, 1917, 1920, 1922, 1924, 1927, 1931, 1935, 1942, 1955, 1960, 1963, 1966, 1975
Robertson Bros.	1942, 1945, 1947, 1955
Royal Oporto Wine Co.	1934, 1945, 1958, 1960, 1962, 1963, 1967, 1970, 1975
Sandeman	1870, 1872, 1873, 1875, 1878, 1880, 1881, 1884, 1887, 1890, 1892, 1894, 1896, 1897, 1900, 1904, 1908, 1911, 1912, 1917, 1920, 1927, 1934, 1935, 1942, 1943, 1945, 1947, 1950, 1955, 1957, 1958, 1960, 1962, 1963, 1966, 1967, 1970, 1975
Smith Woodhouse	1870, 1872, 1873, 1875, 1878, 1880, 1881, 1884, 1887, 1890, 1896, 1897, 1900, 1904, 1908, 1912, 1917, 1920, 1924, 1927, 1935, 1945, 1947, 1950, 1955, 1960, 1963, 1966, 1970, 1975
Sociedade Constantino	1912, 1927, 1935, 1941, 1945, 1947, 1950, 1958, 1966
Southard	1927
Stormonth Tait	1896, 1900, 1904, 1908, 1912, 1920, 1922, 1927
Taylor	1870, 1872, 1873, 1875, 1878, 1881, 1884, 1887, 1890, 1892, 1896, 1900, 1904, 1906, 1908, 1912, 1917, 1920, 1924, 1927, 1935,

	1940, 1942, 1945, 1948, 1955, 1960, 1963, 1966, 1970, 1975
Tuke, Holdsworth (Hunt, Roope & Co.)	1870, 1873, 1874, 1875, 1881, 1884, 1887, 1890, 1892, 1894, 1896, 1900, 1904, 1906, 1908, 1912, 1917, 1920, 1922, 1924, 1927, 1934, 1935, 1943, 1945, 1947, 1950, 1955, 1960, 1963, 1966
van Zeller	1878, 1881, 1884, 1887, 1890, 1892, 1896, 1904, 1908, 1912, 1917, 1922, 1924, 1927, 1935
Warre	1870, 1872, 1875, 1878, 1881, 1884, 1887, 1890, 1894, 1896, 1899, 1900, 1904, 1908, 1912, 1917, 1920, 1922, 1924, 1927, 1931, 1934, 1945, 1947, 1950, 1955, 1958, 1960, 1963, 1966, 1970, 1975
Wiese & Krohn	1927, 1934, 1935, 1947, 1950, 1952, 1960, 1967, 1970

The Register

Although the boundaries of the region had been precisely laid down by 1921, it was only eleven years later that the Federation of the wine-growers of the Douro, better known as the Casa do Douro, came into being. This body consists of all the wine-growers within the limits of the region. At this time it was decided to make a register of all vineyards in the area. The starting point for this ambitious undertaking was a 'Registration of Property', to be completed by the owner, in which the following particulars were given:

owner's name
address
frontages
situation
number of vines
estimated production

The survey of vineyards only got under way in 1937. It was completed eight years later.

The task was entrusted to teams of inspectors under the supervision of a qualified agronomist. Each group comprised an agriculturist, a classifier of vines and a tally-clerk. The teams, which numbered six to eight, worked through the entire region collecting the following data:

a) whereabouts of the vineyard (municipality, parish and location)
b) name and home address of the owner, tenant or acting partner
c) name of the previous owner
d) frontages
e) slopes and water-courses, if any
f) nature of the land
g) inclination of the terrain (in degrees)
h) altitude (minimum, maximum and mean average)
i) average density of planting; height of trellis; pergolas
j) area under plantation, noting area available for further planting
k) condition of the vineyard
l) particular cultural features
m) inter-planted crops
n) age of vines and conditions in vineyard
o) types of vines grown
p) predominant strains
q) percentage of failures
r) other pertinent particulars

Each card on the index had to be signed by the agricultural inspector, the classifier of the vines and the proprietor. The register was always kept up to date, and the requisite number of inspecting teams kept in being to ensure this.

This work is now considered to be the most important of the tasks undertaken by the Federation. To give some idea of its scale, it is enough to say that in 1973 the region boasted, in round figures, no less than 26,000 wine-growers, owning 86,000 properties between them, which, in turn, were planted with 165,500,000 vines.

Note is also made of the age of the vines (one year, two years, three years, between four and twenty-five years, and over twenty-five years old); the kind of soil in which the vines of various ages are growing; the average production and the number of vines grafted or ungrafted.

The principle of Benefit and its distribution

In theory any wine produced within the demarcated region is entitled to be made as Port. In fact, however, owing to the fluctuations of the market and the necessity to maintain the balance between supply and demand, the Port Wine Institute, through its General Council, lays down the amount of wine which is to be given this advantage – in other words the quantity of Port to be made each year.

This figure is arrived at after taking into account the stocks held by shippers and growers, the previous year's figures of exports and home consumption, and the trade's future prospects. Once the amount has been decided on the Casa do Douro is informed so that it can make allocations to the farmers.

In the five years from 1969 to 1973 production of wine averaged 100,925,486 litres, but only 35,304,085 litres were made as Port. So it may be wondered how these allocations are established.

For this purpose the vineyards of the Douro have been classified under a number of headings, to each of which marks are allotted. Based on information obtained by the inspecting teams, an index card is made out for each property. These are then classified on the points system, and those with the higher scores – presumably the producers of the higher-grade wines – will obtain the larger allocations. Thus the distribution of the allowance becomes a safeguard of quality.

It may be well, therefore, to look more closely at the way in which the marks are allotted under the various headings. These are listed in order of importance.

Altitude

This is an important factor and deserves close attention. Within limits, the way in which the region is divided into sections, and these subdivided into sectors, may require adjustment on the grounds of altitude. It may also help to correct the shelter factor, and generally speaking, can be said strongly to affect climatic conditions.

Marks vary between 150 points for vineyards situated at heights of up to 150 metres, and 650 points for those lying between 601 and 625 metres.

Productivity

Various factors come into play here, but there is no doubt that, with rare exceptions, an increase in productivity means a decrease in quality. So it is an important element in assessing the merits or otherwise of a vineyard.

Productivity is naturally strongly affected by the climate, the soil and the quality of the grapes in question, and it often serves to counterbalance marks given or subtracted for situation; its effects on quality have long been recognised, and in the French wine regions it is carefully recorded each year. In the Douro the points allotted for this factor do not change from vintage to vintage; they are, however, periodically reviewed in the light of production figures for each property, which are noted annually. The count for this factor is set out below.

Average production in litres per 1,000 vines	+points	−points
up to 600	120	
600 – 700	90	
701 – 800	60	
801 – 900	30	
901 – 1000	0	
1001 – 1100		50
1101 – 1200		100
1201 – 1300		175
1301 – 1400		250
1401 – 1500		325
1501 – 1600		400
1601 – 1700		550
1701 – 1800		700
over 1800		900

Nature of the land

This hardly calls for comment, since it is obvious that the kind of soil, together with the climate and the type of grape grown, are primarily responsible for the quality of a wine.

Counts here vary between plus 100 for schistous lands and minus 150 for those merging from schist to granite. Granite soils are penalised 350 points, and fertile lowlands, subject to flooding, are graded minus 900.

Locality

For this purpose the region has been divided into five sections, each sub-divided into sectors:

Section 1 comprises the parishes of Mouramorta, Sedielos, Vinhos, Louredo, and the hillsides around Medrões and Fontes which fall away to the valley of the River Sermanha. This section is marked from plus 60 to 0.

Section 2 takes in the region from Barro to the small River Vilar (Fontelo) on the left bank of the Douro, and that from Barqueiros to the River Corgo, on the right bank. This section is divided into twenty-seven sectors, and marks range from a minimum of minus 50 to a maximum of 280 points.

Section 3 is on the left bank of the Douro and takes in the hillsides between the

Vilar and Tedo rivers, and, on the right bank, those between the River Corgo and River Ceira. There are eighteen sub-divisions in this section, and marks vary between plus 50 and plus 460 points.

Section 4 takes in the belt flanked on the west by the Rivers Tedo and Ceira and stretches as far as the Saião. There are thirty-eight sectors in this section. The marks range from minus 50 to plus 600 points.

Section 5 stretches from the Saião to Barca d'Alva. There are fifteen sectors, and marks run from plus 140 to plus 450 points.

The counts here are generally based on climatic considerations – rainfall and temperatures. They tend to rise as one proceeds upstream to the limit of the Atlantic-Mediterranean zone, and to fall away slightly once the Mediterranean zone is reached.

The training of the vines

The way in which the vines are trained – whether along wires in the form of low hedges or on pergolas – has a great influence on how the grapes ripen and on the quality of the resulting musts.

In the first case, the grapes are exposed to the direct rays of the sun and, by night, to the heat reflected from the soil, neither condition applying to grapes grown high over a pergola. So it is to be expected that the former will produce wines of higher quality than the latter; and the respective counts are plus 100 and minus 500.

Varieties of vines

The various types of grape grown in the region are classified as 'Recommended', 'Authorised', and 'Tolerated'. The first category rates a plus value of 150 points, the second of 75 points. The 'Tolerated' varieties score no marks. Unfortunately, there are some varieties which do not fall into any of the above categories. These may be penalised as high as minus 300 points.

Marks are allotted under this heading when the vineyard is inspected for inclusion in the register. Apart from identifying the varieties cultivated, the classifier will estimate the percentage of vines in each category. These are then noted on the card under the heading 'Predominant Varieties'.

Slope

There is no doubt that wines produced from hillside sites are invariably superior to those produced in fields or flat lands. At the same time the hillsides are naturally less fertile than the plains. For this reason, the slope of the terrain has to be taken into account when assessing a vineyard, and marks are given accordingly.

Aspect

When speaking of the natural features of the region, it was explained that the reason for the great variety of grapes grown in the Douro was the variation in climate found between Barqueiros and Barca d'Alva. It was also these climatic differences which led to the area being divided into sections and sectors.

The same consideration has made it necessary to take into account the aspect of a vineyard, the effects of which vary from one section to another. For while in a temperate situation there will be considerable difference in the way the grapes mature on a south- or north-facing slope, this is no longer true of the hotter and less humid lands. Although, in general, a southern aspect is to be preferred, it must also be remembered that in exceptionally hot years the northern slopes may ripen the fruit more perfectly. For this reason aspect cannot be considered a factor of prime importance.

Vineyards in the different sections are assessed for aspect according to the following table:

Section	South	SW	W	SE	E	NW	NE	North
1	10	5	− 5	− 5	−15	−15	−25	−30
2	60	55	45	45	25	30	15	−10
3	90	80	70	70	75	50	35	30
4	100	95	90	90	70	75	65	60
5	90	80	70	70	50	55	45	40

Density of Planting

It is obvious that the density of planting will affect the growth and expansion of the vines, since the lower the density, the greater the area on which the plant can feed and develop. By extension, though within certain limits, increased expansion leads to greater productivity and this in turn to a loss of quality. It is understandable, therefore, that this factor should be included in the assessment of a property.

The densities traditionally found in the Douro region vary between 5,700 and 6,900 vines per hectare. Within this bracket no marks are given. Vineyards planted with more than 6,900 roots per hectare are rated minus 50, and those with less than 5,700 roots per hectare score 50 points.

Soil and degree of stoniness

When we come to look at the question of soil in the Douro, it will be found that this hardly exists, as such. It has been made up of repeated working and trenching, and the land always contains a greater or lesser amount of stone. The degree of stoniness has a marked influence on the supply of water to the vines, which is greater in the more stony soils. It also influences the temperature of the soil in depth. This is also greater in shaly soil where the heat can penetrate more easily. Finally it helps to control extremes of temperature, since stony lands that have absorbed more heat during the day give off this warmth, little by little, at night.

Under this heading, lands are classified as 'very shaly', 'averagely shaly' and 'hardly or not at all shaly'. The first group receives a bonus of 80 points, the second of 40 points, the third is unmarked.

Age of the vines

The vines of each property are listed according to age – the number of plants of one, two, three, four and five years, those of between five and twenty-five years, and those of over twenty-five years being carefully recorded. This is done because young vines produce unequal wines, often of poor quality, whereas grapes from the older stock, or even very old roots, make more balanced wines.

Shelter

Shelter from wind, more particularly cold winds, has a considerable influence on quality. Vineyards are therefore classified as (a) 'very sheltered', (b) 'sheltered', and (c) 'hardly or not at all sheltered'. The corresponding marks are 60 points, 30 points and 0 points.

Correlation of factors

The following table shows the spread of the marks allotted under each of the foregoing headings. The percentage of the total claimed by each section gives some idea of its relative importance.

Factors considered	Minimum points	Maximum points	Spread	%
Altitude	−900	150	1,050	20.6
Productivity	−900	120	1,020	20.0
Nature of the land	−600	100	700	13.7
Locality	− 50	600	650	12.7
Methods of training vines	−500	100	600	11.8
Qualities of grapes	−300	150	450	8.8
Slope	−100	100	200	3.9
Aspect	− 30	100	130	2.5
Density	− 50	50	100	1.9
Soil and degree of stoniness	0	80	80	1.6
Age of vines	0	70	70	1.3
Shelter	0	60	60	1.2
Totals	3,430	1,680	5,110	100

These figures show altitude, productivity, the nature of the land, locality, and method of cultivation to be of primary importance, with the varieties of grape grown and the slope of the vineyard as secondary considerations, and the shaliness of the soil, density of planting, shelter and the age of the vines as tertiary factors. If, however, to the variety of grape are added related elements such as productivity (allowing this one third of its total value, since the other two thirds must be linked with soil and climate), method of cultivation, the age of the vines and density of planting, the figures read somewhat differently:

VINES	%
Varieties	8.8
Productivity	6.6
Method of Cultivation	11.8
Age of Vines	1.3
Density of Planting	1.9
	30.4

LAND	%
Nature of the land	13.7
Slope	3.9
Stoniness	1.6
Productivity (1/3)	6.6
25.8

CLIMATE	%
Altitude	20.6
Locality	12.7
Productivity (1/3)	6.6
Aspect	2.5
Shelter	1.2
43.6

Total 99.8

From this reading we find that the nature of the land rates 25.8% of the total, the vines and allied elements 30.4%, and that the climatic factors bulk largest with 43.6%. This is understandable when it is borne in mind that it is the properties of a single region which are being classified, rather than wine-growing regions which are being compared. In the latter case, the factors relating to the vines and the land would need to be evaluated on a different system.

Given that the ground is, generally speaking, schistous, and that the varieties of grapes do not change, it is natural that the climatic factors should form the main basis for a classification of this sort.

Once marks have been allotted, the properties are grouped in classes, according to their totals:

Class A over 1,200 points
Class B 1,001 – 1,200 points
Class C 801 – 1,000 points
Class D 601 – 800 points
Class E 401 – 600 points
Class F 201 – 400 points

No claim to perfection is made for the points system as here described. All that can be said is that it has been in use since 1948, albeit on occasions with some modifications which have not really changed its nature. We may also claim that, as a method of classification, it is unique, and one that makes it possible to trim annual production in the demarcated region to suit the demands of the market and the general economy of the Port trade.

In this chapter it only remains to describe how the amount of wine fixed annually by the Port Wine Institute to be made into Port is parcelled out among the wine-growers.

In July of each year the Casa do Douro receives applications from the growers for the right to benefit under the allowance. These list the name of the petitioner, the municipality and parish to which each property belongs, the names of the properties, the number of vines of more than four years old, the estimated production, and the amount of wine for which the right of benefit is requested. The applications are then studied and checked against the register which will show to which class each property belongs.

On this basis, the co-efficient of the allowance per thousand vines, depending on the class of the vineyard, can be calculated in the light of the amount authorised by the Institute. This task falls to the Casa do Douro. The co-efficient naturally varies according to the class of the vineyard, the total amount of the allowance for the year, and the prospects of a more or less abundant vintage. However small the allowance for the year may be, vineyards graded as Class A will be allowed to make all their wine as Port.

By way of example, the average benefit granted to each class of vineyard over the decade 1963–1973 is set out below. The total quantity authorised under the allowance was 29,865 hectolitres. The figure is in terms of per thousand vines.

Class A   595 litres
Class B   580 litres
Class C   467 litres
Class D   300 litres
Class E   175 litres

The main varieties of vines grown in the demarcated Port Wine region

RECOMMENDED

Red
Bastardo
Donzelinho Tinto
Mourisco
Tinto Cão
Tinta Francisca
Tinta Roriz
Touriga Francesa
Touriga Nacional

White
Donzelinho
Esgana-Cão
Folgasão
Gouveio or Verdelho
Malvasia Fina
Rabigato
Viosinho

AUTHORISED

Red
Cornifesto
Malvasia Preta
Mourisco de Semente
Periquita
Rufete
Samarrinho
Tinta Amarela
Tinta da Barca
Tinto Barroco
Touriga Brasileira

White
Arinto
Boal
Cercial
Códega
Malvasia Corada
Moscatel Galego

TOLERATED

Red
Alvarelhão
Avesso
Casculho
Castelã
Coucieira
Moreto
Tinta Bairrada
Tinta Carvalha
Tinta Martins

White
Branco sem Nome
Fernão Pires
Malvasia Parda
Pedernão
Praca
Touriga Branca

Autovinification

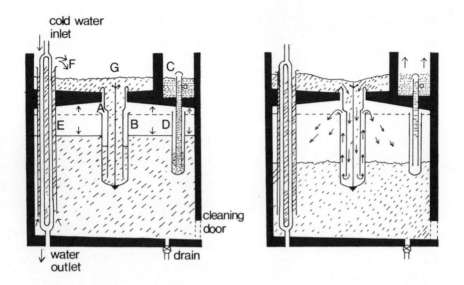

cold water inlet

F G C

A

E B D

cleaning door

water outlet

drain

The vat or cuba consists of a concrete tank, as depicted in Figs. 1 and 2, made of specially treated concrete, normally measuring three cubic metres and mounted on legs. The vat is totally enclosed, the sides extending upwards above the top by about 45 cm. (18 in.). In the left-hand corner is a fibreglass tube (E) open at the top and bottom. It extends above the outside surface of the vat by about 30 cm. (12 in.) and ends about the same distance above the base of the vat. In the vat's centre is a large stainless steel, double, concentric tube of 45 cm. (18 in.) diameter. The outer section (B) is open at the top but closed at the lower end by a ball valve. The inner section is open at both ends, allowing circulation. On the right of the diagram is a similar but smaller concentric tube, the top of which is sited above the upper surface of the vat in an enclosed trough (C). The column is seated on a metal ring at the bottom of this tank. There is a central valve at the top of this tube, called the water control column (D). The draw-off valve and a door giving access to the vat for cleaning are indicated at the bottom of the diagram.

The vat is charged with grapes through opening A, after the double tube has been removed. The outer tube is then replaced with the ball valve open at the bottom to allow the tube to pass more easily into the mass of the grapes. The tube is firmly secured and the valve closed by means of a wing-nut (A).

During fermentation the must liberates carbon dioxide gas. This builds up pressure, which exerts itself between the surface of the must and the underside of the top of the vat. This pressure has the effect of:-

a) making the must rise through tube E. The must rises up the tube and spills over into the enclosed area (G);

b) forcing out the water from the column D, through its valve in tank C. When very little water is left in the bottom of the control column, the CO_2 pressure inside the vat releases itself violently into the outside and projects the remainder of the water into tank C;

c) holding back the must in the column B until the CO_2 has escaped. Otherwise the accumulation of must in area G would return to the interior of the vat prematurely.

At the moment when the gas pressure is released from the interior of the vat, the must which has overflowed into the area G is no longer in equilibrium. By sheer weight it pours down the centre of the double tube A and up the outer jacket with considerable speed, spraying the 'manta' or solid surface of the must, thus completely saturating it and breaking it up (Fig. 2). The water column in the meantime, having allowed all the CO_2 to escape, refills itself again with the correct amount of water from the trough C and then the cycle recommences.

The duration of each cycle depends upon the rate of fermentation and the volume of the contents of the vat, but is usually ten to twenty minutes. It is repeated about 100 to 150 times during the fermentation period and in that short time will extract the maximum colour from the skins.

The tube at the left of the diagram may be fitted with cooling tubes (F). These would be used if the outside temperature was excessive and will slow down the rate of fermentation. The coolant will pass through the tubes from top to bottom, flowing in the opposite direction to the must. They are seldom utilised in the Douro, but this type of vat originated in Algeria, where high temperatures are a problem during fermentation.

The advantage of this vat is its freedom from faults, being entirely hydraulic. Also it ensures that in the process the must is not subjected to excessive aeration and possible bacterial spoilage.

Select Bibliography

ALLEN, H. WARNER, *The Wines of Portugal,* George Rainbird in association with Michael Joseph, 1953.

AZEVEDO, CORREIA DE, *The Wonderful Douro,* Privately printed.

BOLITHO, HECTOR, *The Wine of the Douro,* Sidgwick & Jackson, London, 1956.

BRADFORD, SARAH, *The Englishman's Wine,* Macmillan, London, 1969.

CAMPBELL, IAN M., *Reminiscences of a Vintner,* Chapman & Hall, London, 1950.

COBB, GERALD, *Oporto Older and Newer,* Privately printed, 1966.

COCKBURN, E. H., *Port Wine and Oporto,* Wine & Spirit Publications, London, 1949.

CONTRIBUTED, *A Guide to Good Wine,* W. & R. Chambers Ltd., London, 1952.

CRAWFURD, OSWALD, *Portugal Old and New,* Kegan Paul Trench & Co., London, 1880.

HEALEY, MAURICE, *Stay me with Flagons,* Michael Joseph, London, 1940.

MERLE, IRIS, *Portuguese Panorama,* Ouzel Press, London, 1958.

RAY, CYRIL, *The House of Warre,* Privately printed, 1971.

SANCEAU, ELAINE, *The British Factory Oporto,* Cia. Editora do Minho, Barcelos, 1970.

SANDEMAN, P. W., *Port and Sherry,* Lund Humphries & Co., Ltd., 1955.

SELLERS, CHARLES, *Oporto Old and New,* Howard & Jones, London, 1899.

SIMON, ANDRÉ L., *Port,* Constable & Co., Ltd., London, 1934.

TAIT, GEOFFREY M., *Port: From the Vine to the Glass,* S. Straker & Sons Ltd., London, 1936.

VALENTE-PERFEITO, J. C., *Let's Talk about Port,* J. R. Gonçalves Ltd., Oporto, 1948.

Glossary

ARMAZEM The warehouse above ground in which Port is stored and matured in Vila Nova de Gaia. In English this is termed 'lodge'.

BACALHAU Dried codfish.

BAGA Sweet concentrate of elderberries. Since the eighteenth century no elderberry trees have been grown in the Douro district. Prior to the 1750s elderberry juice was used illegally to increase the colour of the must.

BAGAÇEIRA A marc or grape spirit produced from the distillation of the pressed pomace.

BARCO RABELO A boat peculiar to the Douro river, propelled either by sail or long sweeps of an oar.

BAUMÉ A scale of calibration for hydrometers used in wine-making. 10° baumé is equivalent to a specific gravity of 1.074.

BEESWING A late precipitation of the solids forming the crust in Vintage Port, which have failed to adhere to the existing crust.

BENTONITE Naturally occuring clay-like earth, containing montmorillonite derived from airborne volcanic ash.

BLIND TASTING The samples to be tasted are not necessarily in front of their bottles. The taster cannot therefore identify the sample and must make an unbiased judgement.

BOND, IN BOND or BONDED The storage of wine in the country of consumption before duty is paid. The warehousekeeper deposits a bond or surety with the customs authorities of that country.

BRANDED PORT Wine under a registered name with or without the shipper's name usually promoted by the brand owner.

BURNAY SALE The great sale of Port organised by Southards in 1892 with Burnay & Co. as the bankers.

CASA DO DOURO The guild to which all Douro farmers must belong.

CASEIN The principal protein of milk and cheese. It is purified from skimmed milk by precipitation with acid and sold in powder or granular form.

CHEIA Flooding in the River Douro.

CORGO, CIMA and BAIXO The river which runs into the Douro from the north, to the east of which is the Cima (upper) Corgo, the fine wine area, and to the west the Baixo (lower) Corgo.

CRUST The deposit thrown by wine in bottle.

DEJUICER A mechanical or static device to encourage the separation by draining, of juice from grape skins and other solids.

ENTREPOSTO The area of Vila Nova de Gaia prescribed by law which contains the lodges in which Port must be stored.

EXTRACT The extract of a wine is the alcohol-free, soluble solids and is made up of salts of tartaric acid, malic, lactic and succinic acids, glycerol, tannin, protein and other nitrogenous compounds and sugar.

FACTORY HOUSE   The headquarters in Oporto of the British Association.

FINING   A method of clarifying wine: in order to remove any deposit in the wine, finings of a gelatin or similar basis are added to it.

FREEZING POINT   This depends on the alcoholic strength of the wine and its extract. The greater the strength and extract the lower the freezing point.

GAY-LUSSAC   Degrees of alcohol by volume.

GEROPIGA   Sweet Port used in blending. Made by fermenting the must for a shorter time than usual thus retaining the sugar in the wine.

GREMIO   A guild of traders in one particular trade.

HOGSHEAD   A cask in which wine was exported, containing approximately 58 gallons (half a pipe).

HYDROMETER   An instrument used for determining the specific gravity of liquids, made of glass, brass or lignum vitae.

INSTITUTO DO VINHO DO PORTO   The governing board of the Port Wine Trade in Oporto, on which both the Portuguese Government and Shippers are represented.

KIESELGUHR   A diatomaceous earth, used in the filtration of some wines.

LAGAR   The stone trough in which grapes are trodden in the Douro district.

LANDING AGE   The extra ageing of wine in wood in the country of consumption.

LEES   Residual deposit left in a cask after racking.

LEIXOÊS   The artificially-made harbour north of Oporto whence now nearly all wine is shipped.

LODGE   *See* ARMAZEM

LOT or LOTE   A quantity of the same type and style of blended Port to be used in a shipper's particular mark.

MATCH (MATCHING)   The art of the taster in blending a Port to follow the wine of another shipper.

MUST   Grape juice in the process of transformation into wine.

MOVIMOSTO   A combined pump and paddle worked by electricity used at vintage time in a lagar, replacing the use of the human foot in getting fermentation started and continued as long as required. The pump serves to circulate the must from the bottom of the lagar over the pomace.

PIPE   Bulk Port is usually quoted per pipe. The standard oak cask of the Port trade contains approximately 117 gallons, 534 litres or 56 dozen bottles.

PHYLLOXERA   The aphid originating in America which devastated the vineyards of Europe towards the end of the last century.

POMACE   Stalks, skins, pips and solid matter from crushed grapes.

PORT TONGS   These are used to take the neck off old bottled Port.

PORT WINE TRADE ASSOCIATION   The Association of Port Importers and Agents in the U.K.

QUINTA   A property or farm, usually meaning a vineyard when spoken of in connection with wine.

RACKING   The transfer of wine from one container to another and the removal of lees.

REFRACTOMETER   An optical instrument to measure the refractive index of a liquid. Using conversion tables the refractive index can be converted into density readings.

RECTIFY   Referring to a neutral spirit produced by distillation in a still equipped to separate higher alcohols.

SELO DE GUARANTIA   Seal of Guarantee. The numbered paper seal over the top of the bottle to denote a Port bottled in Portugal.

SPLASH   The white mark on the side of a bottle of Vintage Port denoting which side up it has been binned.

VASLIN-TYPE PRESS   Horizontal basket press with a system of internal chains which break up the pomace automatically after the first pressing, so that subsequent pressing can take place.

VILA NOVA DE GAIA   The town on the south bank of the Douro facing Oporto housing the Port lodges. *See* ENTREPOSTO.

VINHO DO PORTO   Wine of Porto; Port wine.

Index